THE MODERN TEEN'S
ETIQUETTE PLAYBOOK

ALLA KESSER GROSS

**The Modern Teen's Etiquette Playbook:
Confidence, Communication, and
Online Presence for the 21st Century**

Absolute Author Publishing House

https://absoluteauthorpublishinghouse.com

Copyright © 2023

All rights are protected. Unauthorized reproduction, in whole or in part, in any form is strictly prohibited. For inquiries, please contact:

LLUXXALL LLC

office@lluxxall.com

For additional copies or bulk purchases visit:

www.lluxxall.com

Editor: Catharine Kaufman

Book Design: Vlada Ivashchuk

Illustrator: Iryna Prokopchuk

Author Style and Photo: Creative Studio Viktoryia Miller

Paperback ISBN: 978-1-64953-930-4

Hardcover ISBN: 978-1-64953-947-2

eBook ISBN: 978-1-64953-931-1

Printed in the United States of America

DEDICATION

Lovingly inscribed in memory of my parents, Lora and Vova, who instilled in me the values of courtesy, decorum, and compassion. And to my teenage son Areli, and my two stepsons, Sammy and Jay, the driving force behind this endeavor.

CONTENTS

PREFACE

SECTION ONE:
AN INTRODUCTION TO ETIQUETTE

CHAPTER ONE: THE HISTORY OF ETIQUETTE　　2

SECTION TWO:
ALL ABOUT YOU

CHAPTER TWO: LOOKING AFTER YOURSELF CHAPTER　　14
CHAPTER THREE: WAYS OF SELF-IMPROVEMENT　　44

SECTION THREE:
GETTING OUT THERE

CHAPTER FOUR: NICE TO MEET YOU!　　60

SECTION FOUR:
LET'S EAT AND BE MERRY!

CHAPTER FIVE: TABLE SETTINGS　　77
CHAPTER SIX: SERVICE　　80
CHAPTER SEVEN: FOOD, GLORIOUS (FORMAL) FOOD　　92
CHAPTER EIGHT: INFORMAL MEALS　　101
CHAPTER NINE: CHITCHAT　　104
CHAPTER TEN: TECHNOLOGY AT THE TABLE　　108

SECTION FIVE:
GETTING INTO DATING

CHAPTER ELEVEN: HOW TO MAKE THE FIRST MOVE	112
CHAPTER TWELVE: BREAKING UP IS HARD TO DO	114
CHAPTER THIRTEEN: GIFTS AND GIVING	116
CHAPTER FOURTEEN: HOW TO BE A GOOD DATE	118
CHAPTER FIFTEEN: THAT FIRST DATE	123

SECTION SIX:
ONLINE ETIQUETTE

CHAPTER SIXTEEN: WRITTEN MATTERS	130
CHAPTER SEVENTEEN: NETIQUETTE	133
CHAPTER EIGHTEEN: TEXTING	138

SECTION SEVEN:
BUILDING A "FUTURE YOU" TO BE PROUD OF

CHAPTER NINETEEN: MINDFUL YOU	144
CHAPTER TWENTY: PLANNING FOR FUTURE WORK	152

THE AUTHOR	157

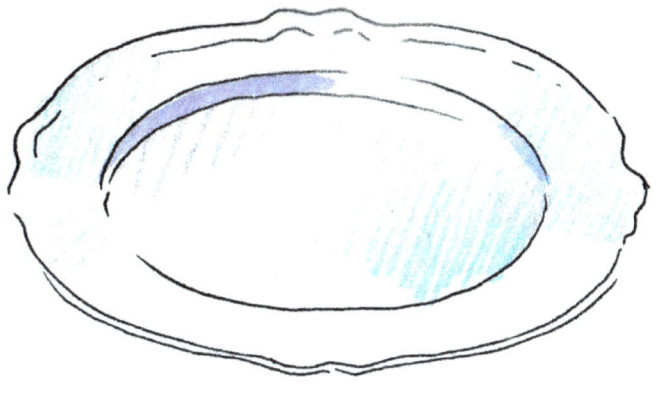

Preface

Have you ever felt unsure of what is expected of you when you find yourself in an unfamiliar setting, whether it is a party, a sports event, or a meal at a fancy restaurant?

Do you sometimes feel as though it seems everyone else has inside information on a given situation and that there must be a secret rulebook floating around that has somehow passed you by?

Well, first of all, everyone feels that way at one time or another—it's very normal, especially if you're working on expanding your comfort zone and putting yourself "out there" into unfamiliar situations to network and get yourself noticed by those who can help you do well in life.

And, secondly—you're right. There are rulebooks floating around (hint: you're holding one right now), but they aren't especially *secret*, as such. It's hard to know they exist when you haven't been told about them. Remember the saying about "unknown unknowns"?[1] The world of etiquette can be an unknown unknown for a great many young people. And, unfortunately, this means that a lot of people will go through their lives unsure if they're doing the right things in any given situation, sometimes being told they are "rough around the edges," "unpolished," or "unmannerly"—quite unfairly, as no one has ever taught them properly what they should be doing instead!

---

[1] "There are known knowns. These are things we know that we know. There are known unknowns. That is to say, there are things that we know we don't know. But there are also unknown unknowns. These are things we don't know we don't know." Donald Rumsfeld, two-time Secretary of Defense (making him both the oldest and the youngest Secretary of Defense in US history!) (There are probably also things we know without realizing it—the unknown knowns! But we won't go into that now.)

Whether you've experienced this sort of unfair judgment, or simply dread having it happen to you, it may have already kept you from trying new things, preventing you from attending "fancy" events, or worrying about feeling awkward in venues that turned out to be classier than you were perhaps expecting.

It might even have kept you firmly glued within your comfort zone, not daring to step outside your safety bubble for fear of doing something "wrong" and being sneered at or embarrassed in some way.[2]

---

[2] A note here about being made to feel as though you don't belong, or that you are intruding where you're not wanted: this is the precise opposite of what systems of etiquette were intended to do!

Anyone who is rude to you or judges you for not knowing something you have never been in a position to learn, is breaching their very own system of manners. While this might not help you at the time when you have no idea what to say or do, later on, when you've recovered your equilibrium a little, you can look yourself in the mirror and say, "They were wrong to treat me that way. It was very rude and a terrible breach of etiquette!"

And that might help you feel a bit better about it all.

But this book is here to save you from all that stress and fear of humiliation! It's a fairly comprehensive guide you can read from cover to cover, absorbing every word—or that you can dip in and out of, consulting it when a specific occasion is coming up and you're not quite sure how to dress or behave. Use it the way that suits your needs and learning style best and you'll soon be able to keep your head up and back straight, even in the most unfamiliar settings.

Etiquette began, as we will see, with the aristocracy in Europe, but gradually trickled through the population and became something for everyone to aspire to. In the USA, there's never really been a hard and fast class system, but there definitely was a system of etiquette in the 1800s and 1900s—a system that gradually came to be seen as obsolete.

In the late 1900s and even into the 2000s, life just became busier and busier, and all these systems of manners and the strict social hierarchies eventually melted away, and parents began to focus on education and other aspects of life instead of pretty manners that didn't seem to have any place in the modern world.

In time, parents no longer taught etiquette for the very simple reason that they were never taught it themselves, nor did they have a copy of this book handy to help them! One of the reasons for the decreased interest in books of manners is that new factors have presented themselves as being much more pertinent: your schooling, for example—earning good grades so you can get into a top-rated college or university. In short, etiquette slid to the back burner of life.

But ironically, good etiquette will open doors for you, making it easier to achieve your goals with inner confidence as you proceed through life impressing all those you meet along the way. So, make sure you keep this book handy as you travel along life's highways and byways.

As an example of good etiquette and how it can help you, let's say you're invited to interview for your dream job over lunch at an upscale restaurant. From educating you on what you should wear, including your clothes, jewelry, and even makeup, to which knife and fork you should use with which dish, this book has all the answers. In most cases, the rule of thumb says to start with the cutlery on the outside and work your way in, and this should apply no matter what dishes are served, as the servers who laid out the cutlery will be aware of what's to be served later and in what order the courses will come out to the diners. But we will delve into the details of fine dining a little later. The point here is to say that the whole structure of etiquette is designed around kindness and inclusivity—once you know to start with the outermost knife and fork and work your way in, you can deal with any place setting that arises because this knowledge offers an easy system to help those not "in the know" navigate everything from meals to conversations to formal balls.

And if you apply this simple "cheat code" to every aspect of life, well, you can see how easy it becomes to make the right decisions with confidence.

Sadly, schools no longer teach etiquette as your teachers' entire focus throughout your schooling is aimed at ensuring you and your classmates meet all the requirements for passing the various classes and getting into colleges or venturing into the real world—both of which, absurdly, can have higher standards of expected behavior despite the absence of teaching these standards in the initial curricula!

So, why is there still a need for people to understand what good etiquette is and why it should be practiced whenever possible instead of just allowing people to behave however they like?

The short answer: good etiquette can steer you safely through interviews and social occasions, see you hold your own in unequal situations, and generally help you steer a smooth course through life, avoiding the bumps and pitfalls of poor decisions and improper behavior.

And now that you own this little etiquette guide—The Playbook for Modern Teens—you will soon learn how to seamlessly fit into any social occasion without embarrassment or drawing unwanted attention to yourself. In fact, you could say that this book has already saved your social life. So read on and find out how.

SECTION ONE:
AN INTRODUCTION TO ETIQUETTE

Chapter One:
The History of Etiquette

The world is changing fast, and with it, people's expectations are changing too. In our recently isolated world where a person can live entirely at home and where school or work can be accomplished online, as can grocery shopping, takeout orders, and even social events, it's all too easy to wonder if there's any need to lay out the rules of engagement regarding in-person communications.

The short answer is—*yes*, there is a need for a system of manners by which you can attend events and meet new people without causing offense or raising eyebrows. Ultimately, there is still a place for etiquette in society.

So, what is etiquette exactly?

A short history lesson follows.

Back in the French court of King Louis XIV (XIV means fourteenth, and in French, Louis is pronounced "Loo-ey") in the 1600s and early 1700s, the king got a bit fed up with people trampling all over his carefully manicured lawn, touching his priceless artwork, and generally behaving in a way he considered rude or "gauche" as the French would say.

But, conceding that they probably didn't know any better, he decided to help them by leaving polite written notices in appropriate places: "Please stay off the grass," for example, or "Please do not touch" on the priceless, porcelain ornaments. These little notices were called "*étiquettes*," which translates to "labels."

From these early labels, gradually, people came to understand how to behave around statues and lawns, and so on, and eventually a system of courtly manners was drawn up—a guidebook on how to behave at court. And pretty soon, nobles and wannabe nobles were all busily teaching themselves and their children how to have refined manners, and how to behave properly should they be lucky enough to socialize in aristocratic circles.

The French Revolution, bubbling and brewing and about to erupt about a hundred years later in the 1790s when the population proved (rather gruesomely) that they could get on with their lives very well if the French royal family no longer existed.

This was a very dark time in France, where anyone suspected of being an "*aristo*" (a noble) was sent to the guillotine to be beheaded, along with any regular citizens who might have protected the former lords and ladies. As always in these troubled times in human existence, it is almost certain that many innocent people were unfairly accused of being sympathizers and maybe even executed. Fortunately, things calmed down after fifteen or twenty years, and France became a settled and civilized country again, replacing the monarchy with a republic.

One thing that managed to survive this purge of the nobility was the system of courtly manners, now known as etiquette, after those earliest labels. Etiquette was well established as a system of politeness for anyone who wanted to be thought genteel and couth, and it continued to be a measure of a person's politeness and civility. One of the reasons for this was that etiquette had already spread to other countries.

> FUN FACT: *The French word étiquette assimilated into the English language, not once but twice. It gave us "etiquette," which is the subject of this book, and also the word "ticket" (remember those labels?).*

Before the French Revolution—indeed, probably fairly soon after Louis XIV had created his little labels—the idea of etiquette as a system of manners and advice on how to behave crossed the English Channel and took hold in the UK.

English society was based upon a strict hierarchy of class, similar to pre-revolutionary France, and the upper crust was enamored with everything French. It was seen as the "in" cool place, and French fashions in clothing, coiffure (hairdressing and styling), and, of course, manners, were quickly adopted by Londoners and embraced as a symbol of being *"en vogue"* (trendy).

And, as the history books tell us, the United Kingdom set out to colonize as much of the world as possible, and all those young, eager noblemen who wanted to both explore the world and make their mark upon it traveled with their ingrained systems of manners and etiquette to places as far away as Africa, India, and, of course, America. It's safe to say that once this happened etiquette's future was sealed—at least for a hundred years or so.

So, etiquette is a "system of proscribed behavior"—which basically means it's a list of things to do or not do in order to be considered polite and proper. Some points of etiquette are obvious and don't really need to be written down, but others can be a little more complicated and will benefit from explanations as to why some behaviors or actions are rude, while others are perfectly acceptable.

Etiquette should not be confused with mere manners, although they are very similar. Good manners tend to be universal and quite broad, whereas etiquette is specific to certain places and occasions.

For example, while it is always good manners to say "good morning" to people you live and work with, it is not always good etiquette to flash them a beaming grin at the same time.

Norwegians can be quite serious and sometimes unfriendly people, and they find Americans—who have largely been raised to smile politely and show interest and enthusiasm toward others—to be slightly alarming.

So, we can see that good etiquette might request Americans to tone down their "good morning" greetings when visiting Norway, while conversely, it would encourage Norwegians visiting America to introduce some warmth and friendliness into their interactions.

FUN FACT: *In Thailand, the royal family is revered, while at the same time feet are considered dirty. So, should someone drop a Thai banknote and have it blow away in the wind, take care not to do what might be instinctive in the United States and stomp on it to hold it in place. This action would be considered a mortal insult to the royal family (whose faces are printed on the banknotes) and would definitely be a breach of Thai etiquette.*

As we saw earlier, etiquette started out as a system of courtly manners used mainly by lords and ladies and those who wanted to be accepted by the upper echelons of society. But etiquette has not remained the sole property of the superrich and titled. Everyone can use etiquette to help them succeed in life in scenarios of all manners.

One important thing to remember as you read through this book is that systems of manners and etiquette did not arise through snobbishness and the desire to "show oneself" to be better than others.

Rather, as mentioned in the introduction, etiquette emerged as a way to ensure that everyone found themselves on a level playing field when faced with an unexpected situation. Instead, like pieces in a sports training kit, etiquette gives you a set of tools and coping mechanisms that will guide you through almost any situation you might face. Think of the acquisition of good etiquette as being similar to staying healthy and eating right, working hard in school, and gathering qualifications; all these things, etiquette included, will help you navigate smoothly through life's journey.

Not only can etiquette help you present a polished and confident persona to strangers you're hoping to impress, but it can teach you how to avoid dicey situations, such as entering someone's property. There is a wrong way and a right way, which can be the difference between committing trespassing, which is a misdemeanor criminal offense, and being invited by the owner to join him or her for a glass of lemonade and an interesting chat.

But perhaps the best thing about possessing good knowledge of rules of etiquette is that it can help you personally! Good etiquette can alleviate anxiety, especially about social events; it can boost your confidence, and it can also encourage you to make the best of yourself, no matter the occasion. This makes so much sense if you think about all the times you've felt uncertain or anxious about plunging into unknown situations. The greatest cause of anxiety is fear of the unknown, and a good understanding of etiquette can help a lot of that "unknown-ness" disappear. You will know what to say if someone asks you a question you'd rather not answer; you will know exactly what that strange, green foam on your plate is (and more importantly, how to consume it!), and you will know what is happening when the host stands and raises their glass to get everyone's attention (almost certainly, he or she is about to make a toast to celebrate whatever the event is about). But etiquette is not only about special occasions and fancy events—it can help you every single day as you go about your life.

Now that you know what etiquette is, and why it's still relevant in today's world, let's begin your initiation into being a politer, more successful, you!

SECTION TWO:
ALL ABOUT YOU

Chapter two:
Looking after yourself

You might be scratching your head a little, seeing this chapter title. What on earth do your personal hygiene habits have to do with knowing which fork to use to eat your cake at a fancy event?

Quite a lot, actually! Just as greeting people politely, using the correct cutlery, and chewing with your mouth closed are considered polite, so is presenting the best possible version of yourself to the world.

In fact, it works both ways. Just as being clean and well-groomed is a form of self-care, so is learning the basics of etiquette—it's all to do with making the best of yourself. And, on the other hand, just as knowing how to keep up a good flow of chitchat without making anyone feel uncomfortable is a desirable trait, being clean and well-presented can do the same thing.

Another way to look at it, especially if you're shy, is to tell yourself that good hygiene and a neat appearance are excellent camouflage. You won't draw unwanted attention to yourself if you fit in—and remember, that is exactly why the first rules of etiquette were drawn up!

So, yes, it is good etiquette to look after yourself. Bathe regularly, keep your hair clean and well-groomed, and make sure your clothes are neat and clean when you go out. Eating right (avoiding anything that might make you feel ill) and getting sufficient exercise for continued good health are all part of making sure you are always at your best and in a presentable state for any occasion that might arise.

Please note, this does not mean you must spend hours making sure your appearance is always flawless and "Insta-ready" with lots of makeup concealing anything you might consider a flaw. You can, of course, wear makeup if that's your preference, but there is no insistence on it if you prefer to maintain a more natural look.

You may have heard the saying— "Your body is a temple," and while you don't have to worship yourself in the mirror, your body is the place where you spend all your time—you may as well make sure it looks good and feels comfortable!

Not only will you be happier with your own appearance, but others will see that you're the kind of person who makes an effort to look nice and fit in. They will appreciate this, which can make them kinder and more welcoming to you than they might otherwise be.

Let's go over the whole body:

- Toes and feet: scrub them in the shower, making sure you get between the toes and under the nails, especially if you've been wearing socks and shoes all day. Feet sweat more than we realize, and if the sweat has nowhere to go, it will just sit on your feet and become . . . unpleasant!

  Sweat can also contain bacteria, which cause a horrible odor when exposed to the air—this is why socks and shoes smell nasty sometimes.

  Toenails are much thicker and sturdier than fingernails, and this can make them tricky to clip neatly. However, a nice, warm bath or shower can soften your toenails a little, making it easier to trim them. Cut toenails straight across, or very lightly follow the curve of your toe, making sure not to allow the free edge of your toenail to become tucked under the skin at the sides—this can cause ingrown toenails which are both painful and unsightly, and can sometimes require minor surgery to repair.

  Use your own personal nail clippers if you can. Manicure sets are quite inexpensive, so there's no reason you should have to share these implements. But, regardless of whether they're shared or not, you should get into the habit of cleaning and sterilizing your grooming products every now and then.

  If you are a swimmer or athlete who spends a lot of time barefoot in damp, steamy, crowded locker rooms, you're at a higher risk of contracting fungal infections such as athlete's foot, which is highly contagious and stubborn to treat. It is much easier to prevent this pesky condition by taking proper precautions. Wear Crocs or slip-ons rather than walk barefoot on the locker room floor; dry your feet very well after showering or swimming; and, if you do get a condition like an athlete's foot, refrain from your favorite sports and hobbies until it has cleared up. This is good etiquette and common courtesy to prevent infecting others with your condition.

- Body Hair: is a very personal matter, and no matter who says what to you, bear this in mind. If you want to remove as much of your body hair as possible, go for it (with a caveat, see below), and likewise, if you don't mind your body hair—or even prefer it—then leave it alone. Many people remove some body hair and leave other areas hirsute, depending on their personal comforts, beliefs (religious or otherwise), and, in some cases, whether or not they feel like making the effort. If you do decide to opt for body hair removal, it can be a good idea to speak to a medical practitioner of some kind (doctor, nurse, or even pharmacist) about the various options available to you, and how to safely test them out. Here are some of the most popular choices:

- Shaving: the pros of shaving are that it is quick and easy to do, gives an instant result, and can even help by exfoliating the skin (making it smooth and fresh) that has been shaved. It does come with some disadvantages, or cons, though. Shaving is quite a harsh process and can scrape delicate skin, and it is possible to cut yourself, creating a wound through which bacteria can enter your bloodstream, potentially (but very rarely) making you very ill. Some people can develop a rash from shaving; this happens when the hair is very coarse, the skin is very delicate, or the skin is dry. You will have to try it out by shaving a small patch of skin and waiting two or three days to see how you react before making a commitment to shaving large areas of skin. To prevent shaving injuries, you should prep the skin using a special shaving gel or cream and choose a razor that is suited to your skin type, especially if you have sensitive skin. You could also use an electric razor which is more forgiving on tender body parts.

- Plucking: mainly used on very small, delicate areas, plucking can be painful, literally bringing tears to your eyes! And it's around the eyes that you'll predominantly use plucking to tidy up unruly eyebrows. With your face, nature usually does a very good job with hairlines and contours, and the mantra "less is more" definitely applies to plucking. Eyebrows are fussy. If over-plucked, they can take ages to grow back, can grow back in a different configuration to the original shape (which can make your face look unfamiliar), and can even grow back lighter, contrary to all the factoids that say hair grows back thicker and darker (it doesn't, it's usually that cut ends are blunt and look thicker than natural "pointed" ends). Use plucking to carefully shape your brow, removing as few hairs as possible, and rely on a little shaping brush and delicately pointed eyebrow pencil to "thicken" sparse patches. Plucking is especially useful for fixing a "unibrow" that can give you an angry look.

- Waxing: using strips of wax-laden paper or cloth is an age-old method of hair removal going back to the days of ancient Egypt, some 3,150-plus years ago! You could say that the Egyptians were the first to value traits that we still consider beautiful today, such as smoothness of skin and firmness of body.

> FUN FACT: *The very first book of manners was written long before Louis XIV. An ancient Egyptian, the vizier Ptahhotep, wrote* The Maxims of Ptahhotep *in the 2370s BC. It was a book extolling, among other things, the virtues of honesty, kindness, and open-mindedness.*

Waxing has changed a little over the centuries, but it is still basically the same technique: a sticky substance is applied to the body and then whisked off again, hopefully taking a swath of unwanted hair with it. Because waxing pulls hairs out by the roots or follicles, it takes longer between treatments (compared to shaving, which needs to be done every two or three days for heavy hair growth), and the new, fine hairs growing through are often lighter and less visible than your original growth, which, again, extends the period that can lapse between treatments. Waxing is quite harsh on your skin though, especially if it's not done correctly, and you should always test any new waxing treatment with a small patch at least twenty-four hours before attempting a full leg (or other area) wax.

- Depilatory Creams: have been around since the mid-1800s and are now very effective, essentially dissolving the hair before you rinse the cream off, leaving behind smooth, soft skin. These creams should only be used on unbroken skin, avoiding cuts and blemishes, and for the recommended length of contact time. Thicker, coarser hairs might need a second treatment, or you might need to combine your depilatory cream with a different hair-removal solution, such as shaving or plucking.

- Laser treatments: these treatments work by sizzling the root of the hair, permanently destroying it over a series of treatments some four to six weeks apart. Laser treatment can be expensive, and it is not guaranteed to work—the hair follicle can survive the treatment which means the hair will regrow. This is especially likely if you don't complete the whole course of treatment. It can also be quite painful, like having a rubber band snapped against your skin, but is said to be not as painful as waxing, and the pain diminishes with each treatment. Make sure you find a reputable and qualified laser hair removal specialist, as it is a minor medical procedure and things can sometimes go wrong. A highly trained specialist will be able to anticipate and prevent problems.

- Electrolysis: this process of hair removal is broadly similar to laser hair removal with a couple of small, but significant differences. Laser treatment works on larger areas of skin at once, destroying several roots at the same time, while electrolysis is much slower but more thorough boasting a higher rate of success in the removal of the hairs and follicles treated. Electrolysis is a slow and fairly painful process, akin to plucking, as it targets one hair at a time, and as such, is best kept for those problem areas like a stubborn tuft on a chin, or a hairy mole. Always consult a doctor before attempting any treatment on odd patches of body hair that occur from time to time, as these can be a sign that there is something brewing under the surface.

Your parents should speak to you about your body as it grows and changes throughout childhood, puberty, and into young adulthood, and this should include advice on things like body hair removal and when you should start doing it. However, human bodies are infinite in their variety and your body may mature faster than your parents expect. It can feel really strange to speak to your parents about things that are going on with your growing body, but just as with anything in life, there are ways to raise these issues in a calm and non-confrontational way. Hopefully, your parents will have anticipated these things, but if they haven't, or if there's anything they haven't tackled that you're anxious about, do speak to them about it. It's all part of growing up, and even the most protective parent doesn't really want you to stay a child forever! Don't be embarrassed about these occurrences; if you have no control over the timing of these, why on earth should you be?

Instead, raise the subject with them calmly and civilly, pointing out that, for example, your underarm hair is growing thickly and that you find it embarrassing at swim meets. Most parents will be mortified that they haven't realized there's a problem or that you're self-conscious about this, and will happily give you permission, supplies, and resources to allow you to remedy the issue immediately. But if you don't explain it to them, they won't know, and therefore will not be able to help.

On that note, we continue moving up your body to your:

- Privates and torso: keep them clean and hygienic, and mostly keep them to yourself! If you're attending a pool party, you may see groups of people changing in front of one another very casually. You do not have to join in with this, especially if you're new to the group, even if it's a same-sex group. There is absolutely nothing wrong with using a modesty cubicle, or waiting until everyone else has changed before stripping yourself. What is a no-no is staring at other people's nudity—and definitely do not comment on anyone else's body, for any reason, even doling out a compliment.

- Armpits: if your armpits are prone to perspiration, use a good quality deodorant to avoid the embarrassment caused by an unpleasant odor. Your armpits deserve a little section to themselves because of the issue of deodorant and antiperspirant, which are, some may be surprised to learn, different things. Deodorants are literally *de-odor-ants*, which means they mask or remove smells. Antiperspirants, again as the name implies, work by preventing you from perspiring or sweating. While the latter may seem like a good thing, it really is not. Your body needs to sweat to maintain your core temperature, reduce salt levels, and much more, and hampering these functions is like trying to stop a water leak by putting a finger over the end of a hose instead of turning it off at the tap; the system will back up and you can develop boils and skin outbreaks that are unsightly, painful, and unhealthy. Antiperspirants work by using aluminum salts to block your apocrine sweat glands—in short, they stop you from sweating under your arms. There are other products on the market, however, aluminum-free deodorants which work to stop your sweat from smelling so strongly and unpleasantly. These deodorants contain antibacterial ingredients that overpower the smell-producing bacteria in your sweat, and often add a pleasant aroma or fragrance over the top of this smell reduction, even if your workout shirt has become damp with sweat.

- Arms and hands: hands should be clean with nails an even length, neatly trimmed and clean. As early as you can, develop the practice of washing your hands appropriately; it is possible to wash them too often, just as it's possible to not wash them enough. As a rule of thumb, wash your hands before and after you eat and drink anything, after every visit to the bathroom, and when coming in from outside. There are activities when more frequent handwashing is necessary—for example, if you're handling raw meat at a barbecue—but make sure it's commensurate with your potential contamination. Sometimes excessive handwashing might be seen as an insult to the host, as though you think their home is dirty, or as an obsessive-compulsive habit. So, it's important to find the right balance.

But it doesn't matter how clean your hands are if your nails are dirty or unkempt. You will not look as clean and polished as you'd like to, and you might still be harboring germs and bacteria in the rough edges of your fingernails or caught underneath your cuticles. The free edge of your fingernail should be trimmed to a sensible length (tending to shorter if you work with your hands a lot) and gently curved to match the curve of your fingertip. If you are prone to splitting nails, consult a nail technician as there are various products that can help to prevent this happening and others that can repair the nail to minimize damage.

- Face and neck: wash your face first thing in the morning, last thing at night, and any time it might need it. These occasions can include after swimming in a chlorinated pool or the sea (both can leave residue on your skin), after you've removed a day's worth of makeup, or after you've been eating particularly messy, handheld food like ribs, pizza slices, or burgers (more on eating gracefully later in the book). But even if you haven't been swimming, you should have a quick and simple skincare regimen: cleanse, moisturize, and use sun protection with a reasonable SPF on your face and neck every day.

If you're in any doubt about trying out a new skin product, you should consult an expert like your dermatologist if you've had skin issues in the past. If you use makeup, you should be careful to remove it all thoroughly before you go to bed or as soon as you can after the event. Use non-comedogenic products with your cleansers and makeup removers to ensure your pores are not blocked and your skin can function as intended. If you do end up with a skin outbreak (spots, rashes, sore patches, zits, or pimples), rather than try to cover them up with makeup or constantly touch them to see if they've gotten bigger or smaller, wash your hands before you touch your face for any reason. Consult a medical professional about any serious issues, and watch what you eat. While the old saying that pimples are caused by too much chocolate has long been debunked, it is true that some foods, especially processed ones and preservatives can have a negative impact on your skin.

- Teeth and Mouth: good oral hygiene is one of the biggest boons of the twenty-first century, and it should be your delight, as well as your duty, to look after your teeth and breath. Ugly, discolored, or rotting teeth do not impress anyone and will make people stay away from you, while bad breath will make them back away from you and can even make other people feel nauseous. Brush your teeth at least twice a day, and floss regularly. Take steps to ensure your teeth are as white as possible with gentle bleaching and as straight as possible with the use of braces. And, to make sure your oral health remains in great condition, visit your dentist or hygienist as often as recommended. An attractive smile is one of the nicest things you can wear! Remember the wonderful line from the Broadway musical Annie, "You're never fully dressed without a smile."

- Hair: style your hair in a flattering way to frame your face, and always clean and as well-groomed as possible. That said, bad hair days do exist, and they happen without warning sometimes!

- Hairstyles should be kept trimmed, and you should always be able to clip up or tie back long hair if needed. Beards and other facial hair should be trimmed and styled neatly, and you should take great care when eating so as not to "feed your beard" and end up with crumbs and fragments hiding out in your hair for hours after the meal! If you're a swimmer, as mentioned above in "Face and Hands," there are special hair care products that will help remove chlorine and other pool care chemicals from your hair and restore its natural shine and hydration levels.

- Avoid using harsh chemical treatments and hot styling tools in your hair. While it might look good temporarily, these items can cause long-term damage to both your hair and scalp. There is a difference between looking your best and having impossible expectations. There is a great range of organic, gentle hair products on the market tailored to a wide variety of hair types, so work out what your hair needs to look its best, and then purchase the kindest products that will help you get there.

- If your hair doesn't fit into any of the "normal" classifications, then book an appointment with a good hairstylist for a consultation to make the most of your crowning glory.

- Hair loss should always be checked with a medical professional, even if it is expected for your age and gender just in case it's a symptom of something more serious.

FUN FACT: *As many as 25 percent of people cannot smell their own body odor, whether it's their armpits, their malodorous feet, or other bodily aromas. While some people do have less of a smell than others, it's always best to assume you might be in that 25 percent and take steps to both prevent and alleviate bodily smells as much as you can.*

Knowing what to wear

Along with being as clean and attractive as possible, you should also have an understanding of appropriate attire for certain occasions. There are thousands of people all over the world who have mortifying memories of turning up to an event and being:

- the only person in a party dress and sandals when everyone else is in shorts or tank tops at a beach party.
- the only person not wearing a suit or sports coat at an event, having arrived in jeans and a T-shirt.
- the only person not in a fancy dress or, arguably much worse, being the only person in a fancy dress.

The reason these misunderstandings arise is clear: people have different ideas about what constitutes, for example, "smart casual", and where the line between that and simply "casual wear" lies. In the 1980s and 1990s, jeans were definitely "casual" and appropriate at barbecues, beach and pool parties, and for very informal, indoor gatherings. A decade or so later, however, jeans were the very epitome of smart casual, especially when paired with a nice shirt and cool shoes, and would no longer raise an eyebrow at most restaurants. As the line has moved, people and places have not moved in perfect step with the times; some places still frown upon jeans, while others welcome them—and it can be really hard to tell which is which.

Unless you have this handy book with you, of course. Let's take a look at some sartorial choices that will ensure you don't make a misstep when dressing to impress.

Some clothing choices are more or less unspoken, and this is exactly why people begin to fall afoul of etiquette expectations, so let's run down a few things that "everyone knows."

Do not wear white or cream to weddings once you're old enough to attend them. People, especially women, who wear white, bridal- or prom-style dresses to other people's weddings are often seen as being envious of the bride and/or wanting to steal some of the attention that should be on the happy couple. (By the way, it's also a no-no to announce an engagement or get engaged at someone else's wedding—even if such a happy event occurs at the wedding, the newly engaged couple should keep it to themselves and make the announcement after the married couple's day. Obviously, as teens, you're most likely not thinking about getting married yet—something to bear in mind for the future). It should also go without saying that no one should play pranks at a wedding; it is a solemn and happy celebration of love that, for some people, will be their only marriage—don't be tempted to ruin it for them just for a chuckle, whether by playing a prank, dressing inappropriately, or by shouting out when the officiant asks if anyone knows why the couple should not be wed.

If you have a job, perhaps for "pocket money," or saving for college, you should dress modestly at work. Even if you love spaghetti-strap dresses or halter necks and booty shorts, keep them for your leisure time. When you are at work, no matter where it is or what kind of work you're doing, dress according to the employee handbook guidelines, and make sure you're decently covered—for your own safety and comfort if nothing else.

Should you be required to attend a government building for any reason, such as when you're applying for your driver's license or getting a passport photo taken, you should dress appropriately in smart clothing with—for preference and best results—a dark, solid-color top. Casual clothing might embarrass you in the future (and passport photos are rarely flattering to begin with!) and can offer a poor impression to the officials who'll be helping you with your needs. It's much better to impress them with a neat appearance.

Personal image

Do you know what your personal style is?
Or, if not, how you can create it?

Your style will predominantly depend on the way you put yourself together. The visual aspect is king when it comes to your own style, although other factors do apply too: the way you feel and carry yourself, for example, and whether or not you like a certain look. But let's begin with your image.

Where do you turn to for fashion inspiration? Here are some ideas:

- Read fashion magazines such as Vogue, Harper's Bazaar, and Elle. They will often feature the latest fashion trends, but they'll also, invariably, contain information about timeless classic outfits. Even if you love to be trendy, take note of these evergreen clothing items.

- Browse online retail sites taking note of the small differences that can transform an outfit: shorter hemlines, for example, or contrasting colors.

- Find a few fashion bloggers and subscribe to their newsletter.

- Start a "fashion" board on your Pinterest account—after you've pinned a few lovely outfits, the app will begin to recommend similar outfits and accessories, helping direct your fashion sense.

- You can also go old school by studying books and archival material about fashion, paying attention to the outfits in classic movies, and seeking out vintage silhouettes to emulate.

- Once you have an idea of fashion houses that cater to your tastes, you can check out their histories—and indeed, research the timeline of fashion.

Search for images of those people who've stood the test of time as style icons, such as, Jacqueline Kennedy, James Dean, Brad Pitt, Zendaya, Emma Chamberlain, Harry Styles, Timothée Chalamet, Christy Turlington, Olivia Rodrigo, the Olsen sisters, Taylor Swift, and Selena Gomez, to name just a few.

Many of the above-named people are not teens, some are no longer with us, but they have all made their mark and remained in the public consciousness as fashion icons, and as such, they can be admired and emulated. The more you immerse yourself in the world of fashion, the more material you have to craft the best version of yourself—or to put it more simply, studying these exemplary people will help you be the best you can be.

Once you have an idea about whose look or style you admire (some might give you an idea about what you don't like, and that's useful too), jot down the answers to the following questions:
- What about their style inspires you?
- What features about them and their outfits do you notice time and time again?
- What accessories or items make them iconic?
- What color palette do they use?
- Pay attention to makeup and/or hairstyles that are their "defaults."

Articulating the answers to these questions will help you to form the basis of your own style.

How to work with your wardrobe and dress appropriately for the occasion

Putting together a well-rounded wardrobe that will stand you in good stead is something everyone can do. Let's start with your literal wardrobe: go through all your clothing, and be brutal. Get rid of anything that is ripped (and can't be mended), you haven't worn in two years or more, permanently stained, too small, or that doesn't raise positive emotions when you look at it.

Next, you must work out how and where you spend the bulk of your time. A weekly schedule is a good place to start, but you can take note of annual events and one-off celebrations. Doing this will help you realize that if you spend most of your time at school and very little at formal, black-tie events (perhaps one per year) then your wardrobe should reflect this same balance. You won't need ten formal evening gowns, but you will perhaps need to invest in some more good jeans or basic knee-length skirts. Don't rush to throw away clothing you're discarding, unless it's in poor condition, ill-fitting, obsolete, or that you've fallen out of love with. These can be gifted to others or exchanged for something that you will love and use.

So, once you've created your schedule, you'll be able to draw up a summary that will look something like this fictional example:

—— Weekly Use of Time Awake ——

School – 60%
Home – 15%
Gym – 5%
Friends – 10%
Family time – 10%

It's easy to see that most of your time is spent at school, while a small amount of time is spent at the gym. Now you can ensure that your wardrobe contains the right proportion of clothes to suit your needs. Begin by going through your newly pruned wardrobe and dividing everything up into the places and occasions for which you wear them.

You have started developing the most important skill in clothing management: *the capsule wardrobe*.

What is a capsule?

A clothing capsule contains a limited number of items, including accessories, that can be incorporated into various outfits. These capsules can help you put together stylish outfits, and they can be a boon when you're in a rush to choose an outfit for the day (or evening). The idea is that all the items in each capsule will go well together, no matter how much you mix and match them.

Most capsules will contain staple items: a pair of black trousers, for example, which can form the basis of many different looks, as well as more interesting items or accessories (such as a gold chain belt) that will add a unique touch. While the basics will remain in their capsule with their complementary companions, the unique items (the belt) can transfer from one capsule to another to add sparkle to a different capsule's basic items, even if that capsule falls into a very different dress code and category.

Another reason for creating wardrobe capsules is to encourage your imagination when it comes to putting outfits together to create your chosen style.

> **PRO TIP:** *Take photos of your capsule items in the various combinations they comprise. This will save you a lot of time when you're dressing up and want to recreate a look you know you loved.*

What suits me?

We are all different, each with our own particular features: body shapes and types, differing heights, hair color and texture, skin tones, and so much more. And this is a good thing—imagine a world where we all looked and dressed exactly alike. It would quickly become very boring.

And everyone can make the most of the body and face they have, especially if they embrace their individuality and learn how to emphasize their best features instead of blindly following fashion.

First of all, have a good look at the raw material you'll be working with. Take a picture of yourself in a mirror, ensuring you capture your whole body in such a way that you can determine your body shape. Examine that photo, trying to be as objective as you can (and yes, it is hard to do!), and find those parts of you that are unique. We should all celebrate the things that are distinctively our own.

Now, let's look at some body types.

—— For Women ——

Compare your selfie with the body shapes below and see which one your body most closely resembles. Do this by comparing shoulder and hip width, your waist compared to your hips—it might take some measuring and care, but you will soon find your body type.

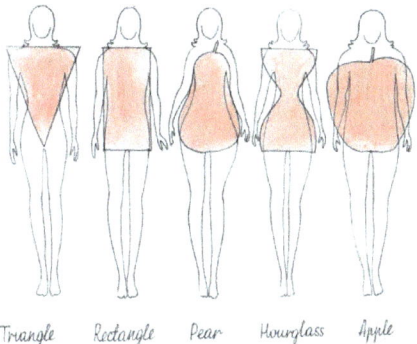

Triangle   Rectangle   Pear   Hourglass   Apple

Once you've found your body type among the five examples above, here are some basic guidelines to follow.

Even though there are five body types depicted, dressing for your body type offers two different groups.

The first consists of hourglass- or pear-shaped bodies.

These body types look best with separates that accentuate the waist and shoulder areas. Tailored outfits made from fabrics with some structure to them are also recommended. For more daring looks, you can choose a bodycon dress, and to disguise any areas you don't especially want to show off you can choose A-line outfits. Trousers and jeans should cinch at the waist rather than start on the hip (as with low-rise waistlines). Baggy or oversized clothing should be assessed to make sure it's appropriate for the occasion.

The second group consists of rectangular, apple-shaped, and inverted-triangle body shapes. The point of the body that will catch the eye is your shoulders, so a nicely tailored or structured shoulder is key, with a number of vertical lines drawing the eye downward. These lines can be created with striped fabrics, but you can also layer your outfit to achieve the same result; vests, shirts, and jackets all offer the narrowing effect that will enhance your image. Jeans and pants should sit at mid-waist, and if you're proud of your legs, you can show them off with miniskirts or dresses, or reveal their shape with skinny jeans. A-line skirts create an interesting and attractive outline and V-neck tops enhance this too.

—— For Men and Unisex ——

Study the body shapes below and ascertain which one best resembles your appearance. As with women, this can be surprisingly difficult, especially if you have not been accustomed to studying your physique objectively before now. Once you have an idea, there are three groups of styling to choose from.

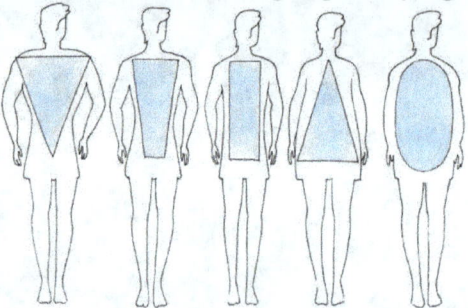

Inverted Triangle   Trapezoid   Rectangle   Triangle   Oval

Rectangle and inverted-triangle figures benefit from straight lines falling from fitted shoulders with generous sleeve allowances. Pants and jeans should be chosen according to your waist measurement and thus be fairly straightforward—but do choose the right length for your legs; overly long trousers bunch up around your feet making you look like a child wearing dad's pants, and too short a pair of trousers make it seem as though you've had an unexpected growth spurt! Semi-fitting clothing is the order of the day, showing off your shape without hugging tightly to any part of it.

Oval body shapes and triangle-shaped bodies can be somewhat lacking in the shoulder area; select clothes with a structured shoulder to enhance this feature. Medium-weight jeans and trousers will balance this out, and stitch details on trousers draw the eye to the whole effect. Avoid oversized jackets and sweaters as these can make your shoulders appear drooping or melting.

Trapezoid body shapes benefit from an enhanced forearm to balance the wide, well-developed shoulders and draw attention to the narrow waist and hips. Shirts can be fitted, while pants and jeans should be straight-legged and semi-fitted called boot-cut.

Once you've assessed your body shape and found the clothing styles that best suit you, along with having a good understanding of which colors best complement your complexion and hair and eye coloring, you should then be able to easily choose garments that will not only suit you, but also fit well into your various wardrobe capsules.

Hairstyles and face shapes

There are six classical face shapes—but people are infinite in their genetic variety. To begin with, you should choose the face shape that's closest to your own so you can make a good decision with your hairstyle or haircut and tweak it to suit your individual style.

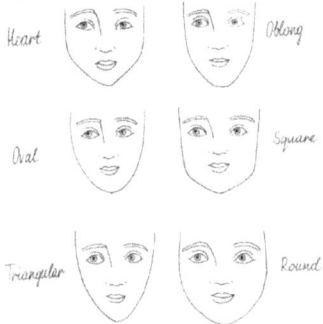

These are the basic face shapes:

Round face

With a round face, the aim is often to soften the roundness with a judicious choice of hairstyle.

—— Women ——

Short – Short crops and pixie cuts that are as short as possible with sharp, uneven strands to break up the look. Women with curly hair should avoid this sort of style.

Mid-length – Allow the hair to flow past the collarbones and brush your shoulders. This style suits most types of hair from curly to straight, and is fairly versatile too.

Long – Long curls flowing down your back, fine hair cut into volumizing layers with shorter strands touching the cheekbones and chin. The latter will have the effect of drawing the roundness in, slimming and lengthening a round face.

—— Men and Unisex/Nonbinary ——

Again, try to lengthen your face by wearing your hair long on top while having it clipped quite short and close on the sides. Experiment with a side parting—go for a middle part if you're feeling bold and have a very symmetrical face. Quiffs (long hair on top with sides tapered), are a great way to add some pizzazz to your appearance.

Triangular face

With triangular faces can often get away with daring styles, but the following are recommended for those seeking a more conventionally neat appearance.

—— Women ——

Short – Balance your narrow chin by adding some volume to the sides. A sleek bob with a heavy fringe can work well. Curls next to your face also add that all-important volume.

Mid-length – A long (to the shoulders) bob works well here. Mix the look up and widen your cheekbones with some oblique bangs.

Long – An evenly cut long fringe or bangs should lead into a good volume of hair (lightly curled if it isn't very thick) falling beside the face down the back.

—— Men and Unisex/Nonbinary ——

Side partings, textured appearance (experiment with gels, gums, clays, and sprays until you find a look you like and that your hair responds well to) and an angular fringe can all add up to an exciting image that flatters your face shape.

Oval face

—— Women ——

Short – Allow curls to flourish the ears or even beyond to the cheekbones. Pixie crops also suit this face shape.

Mid-length – Allow smooth curls, rounded at the ends to sit at shoulder length or slightly longer.

Long – As with mid-length hair, but with the smoothly finished curls falling well below the shoulder. Layered cascade cuts add volume to fine or thin hair.

—— Men and Unisex/Nonbinary ——

This face shape suits a shorter style with side parts, or a smoothly slicked back do. Styling products should be lightweight so as to avoid too much volume on top, which can make the face look disproportionately long.

Square and Rectangle face

—— Women ——

Short – An extreme, short cascade that covers the cheekbones and partly to the chin. The aim here is to add width to the hairline and narrow the lower jaw and chin.

Mid-length – This length is best avoided for those with squared faces as the style broadens the appearance of your face.

Long – Again, add lots of volume at the top before allowing waves to gently descend beyond the shoulders, subtly framing and reshaping the face to suit your preferences.

—— Men and Unisex/Nonbinary ——

Experiment with an edgy undercut and quiffed styles as well as try out differing levels of volume until you find the look you like and that suits your personality.

<u>Heart-shaped face</u>

—— Women ——

Short – Shorter styles can add even more width to an already wide upper half of your face. In general, these styles are not recommended for this face shape.

Mid-length – Severe styles like a blunt-cut bob level with the chin, or a feathered (and slightly longer than usual) pixie crop work well.

Long – Wear your hair to shoulder length, whether straight, wavy, or curled as your hair will simply frame your attractive face shape.

—— Men and Unisex/Nonbinary ——

Add interest and texture by experimenting with fringes, quiffs, and other lightly volumizing styles.

What message do I send when I dress up?

What do you think when you see people out and about, whether in the supermarket or at an event? Each of your capsule looks should make a statement that tells others about your character, frame of mind, or current mood (that is to say, businesslike, informal, ready-for-a-beachside-party kind of moods, not angsty or grumpy moods). The outfit should also express your individual character and personality, and carry a message to society—preferably a good, positive one.

Have you ever felt a little nonchalant about your clothes? Perhaps you're exhausted from working out at the gym or school activities, or just want to lounge around in your comfy clothes—or even your pajamas. But these "non-outfits" also send a message to the people around you, and staying in your pajamas is, perceptually speaking, the same as saying, "I don't respect you enough (or myself) to even get dressed."

However, not every outfit has to be carefully coordinated to send a message. Sometimes your desired message can be carefully neutral; you're neither trying too hard nor ignoring the protocols of etiquette—you are simply being yourself today. And that is absolutely fine.

But on the days that you do want to make a particular impression, you can achieve this by using a number of different styling tools. These include:

- Accessories such as sunglasses (or glasses versus contact lenses), your jewelry choice, shoes or handbag, and so on.

- Clothes that offer a hint of your style: prints and colors that add cheer or produce a somber mood, bagginess to indicate informality, tailoring for formality, and even structured clothing to change your shape, should you wish to.

- The lack of any statement is also a statement.

When you are planning your look—the statement you wish to make with your outfit— return to your capsule wardrobe and experiment with the following:

- You can wear plain and muted (monotone) colors throughout your outfit.

- Choose a statement garment that offers an attractive shape, which you can accentuate by pairing with neutral or muted accessories and shoes so the statement piece pops.

- Use complementary colors with the statement piece to add interest to your outfit. Wearing monotones or one color can be striking and effective, but sometimes it can also miss the mark, so you'll have to try coordinating various separate pieces together to find the best matches. See the color wheel below for harmonious colors (those within the same "quarter" of the wheel), contrasting shades (those opposite each other), and complementary shades (those colors that work well together, despite their placement on the wheel).

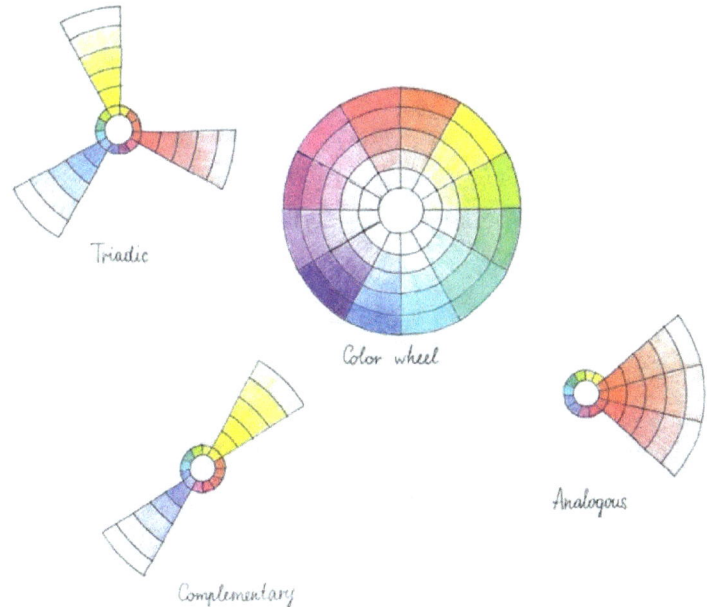

Triadic

Color wheel

Analogous

Complementary

Finally for this section, let's take a look at perfume.

Perfume: a rundown

Do you know the differences between the various fragrances you can find in stores and online?

The way you smell is important on a very profound, almost primeval level. Think of your best cuddling memories with your parents, siblings, or grandparents—anyone that you love. Think of their personal body aromas. For most people, this mere memory is enough to bring a smile to their faces, and that's why choosing the right perfume is so important.

Perfume is just as much a part of your wardrobe as your clothing, and just as you'll change your clothes for different events, you should have an array of perfumes at your disposal to suit your moods and the occasion. Some scents work better for formal evening events, while others are better as a light, everyday fragrance.

When you're first learning about perfumes you might worry about choosing the right scents. Let's have a quick look at how to choose the right scent or scents for your needs.

> FUN FACT: *Back in the old days in the 1700s and 1800s, perfumes contained the animal products castor and ambergris (spit from a sperm whale—yikes!) and they were skin irritants. But this wasn't a problem as people sprayed perfume on their clothing or on handkerchiefs rather than directly on themselves.*

—— How to choose the right scent ——

First of all, do you like it or not? If it doesn't agree with your olfactory or tastes, then don't buy it!

Is it right for you? Some countries have unisex fragrances, whereas in other countries, fragrances are marketed specifically for males or females. (Of course, you don't have to adhere to these categories, but on very formal occasions you might want to conform, even in the small matter of your scent.)

Consider the weather as a fragrance barometer. When it's hot and humid, heavy perfumes can be cloying and overwhelming, and when it is cold, lighter perfumes can get lost in the chill.

Test it thoroughly. Spray some scent on your wrist (a good pulse point) and leave it for an hour or two as you carry on with your day. Then smell your wrist, and if you still like it, wait another three hours or so then repeat your smell test. Still a favorite? Go back and buy it!

Morning scents benefit from being fresh and light, exhilarating and pretty with some sharp high points. These include anything with an aquatic theme, citruses, and florals. You should smile when you catch a whiff of your morning perfume—it should be light-hearted, invigorating, and get you into gear for the day.

Daily scents are those you wear often when you want to give a good impression. Not only should it smell nice to everyone around you, but it should smell just as good to you at the end of a long day as it did first thing in the morning.

While you can absolutely splash on your heaviest perfumes for evening wear be mindful of your venue. Too much strong perfume in a small or enclosed space can be overwhelming, just as it can be in a larger space if there are a lot of people all slathered in their favorite scents! If you're going out to dinner too, watch the heaviness of your perfuming hand. Excessive smells, no matter how expensive or lovely, can interfere with the taste of the food, especially subtle flavors like fish, and it would be a breach of etiquette to ruin a chef's hard work with a thoughtlessly heavy dose of your favorite perfume.

Finally, have a scent that is just for use at home. This is where you can indulge your taste for quirky scents and odd combinations, or you can simply use a scent that makes you feel happy! You don't have to apply your favorite "home" perfume to your skin, rather, you can spray it on your bedding and curtains too for a pleasant waft every time you lounge in bed or open the curtains to start your day.

—— Some rules for perfume use ——

Less is more. That means a little dab will do you, so, don't drench yourself in the stuff! You can always add a little more, but it's impossible to remove excess perfume without washing it off and getting ready all over again.

Apply it to the nape of your neck under your hair. If you know your perfume is very strong, use just a small amount. As it warms up with your body heat the fragrance will disperse around you, keeping you smelling lovely without overwhelming anyone.

If you're one of those people whose skin seems to shed perfume quickly, carry your scent with you and apply just a small spritz when you notice your fragrance fading.

> PRO TIP: *Always ask a friend if they can still smell your perfume. When you are standing with the perfume in your nose for a long time (such as when you're wearing it), it can stop registering. If your friend gives you the thumbs-up, then you can top off your scent.*

Bear in mind that sometimes people commenting on your perfume is not always a complimentary thing. If a lot of people mention your perfume, be savvy to the fact that maybe you've overdone it!

Chapter Three:
Ways of Self-Improvement

Can you walk properly? This might sound like a silly question, but during other eras young people were taught to walk "properly" with a straight back and shoulders, legs swinging forward evenly from the hips. This changed into modern deportment, which literally refers to the way you carry yourself when walking, sitting, or standing. You may have seen or been told about young people, most often girls, being made to walk around a room with a book balanced on top of their heads. Having the book balanced there—you can't touch it!—forces you to keep your head very still as you move, and also evens out your gait, so you glide gracefully around the room, rather than bouncing around like kids in a jumping castle.

FUN FACT: *Victorian governesses used to make the children in their care lie very straight and still in their beds, heads centered on the pillow with their hands straight down by their sides. The idea was to always present a neat and uniform appearance, even when fast asleep!*

You don't have to put a book on your head and walk around for fifteen minutes or so unless you want to, of course, learn how to move smoothly and elegantly the old school way. Instead, you can just practice good deportment by standing and walking tall, making the most of every inch of your height, no matter what that is. Keep your gaze level, looking in front of you, rather than slouching along with your eyes to the ground, or sticking your nose in the air, which can cause you to trip as you're not looking where you are going. Imagine you're carrying a cup and saucer on either shoulder as you walk along, ensuring that your steps are smooth, so you glide effortlessly.

For women, wearing heels can be dicey, but it really is the case that practice makes perfect. When you're wearing flat shoes, whether these are sneakers, loafers, or any flat shoe, you will find that your feet naturally land next to each other as you walk; that is to say, they remain a hip distance apart. Once you add height with a heel, your walk should change so that instead of running parallel to one another, your feet swing in, so your footprints almost form one line rather than two. Do not exaggerate this motion—you're not sashaying along— but keep it natural with a slightly shorter step than you usually take.

High-heeled shoes must fit properly; too loose will cause you to wobble around like a baby gazelle, while too tight will be painful and potentially cause foot problems later in life.

Walking along with a good, head-up posture makes you look more confident, and this can actually boost your self-esteem too!

> FUN FACT: *Faking happy emotions, by, for example, flashing a big smile when it's the last thing you really feel like doing can actually cause a change in your mood, forcing your body to produce "happy" hormones. In other words, if you hold a fake smile for long enough, it becomes real and you actually begin to feel euphoric! Scientists have tested this strange but true phenomenon, and they aren't entirely sure how it works—but they confirm it does. (It also works with body language too: faking confidence and calmness and soon enough you will be.)*

Talking about a chin-up posture, how up is too much? Indulge in a little playacting here: pretend you're a very snobby person with your nose in the air because you are so much better than everyone else. Did you tilt your head almost forty-five degrees in the air, so anyone looking at you could see straight up your nostrils? Yes, that's a poor pose to take making you seem arrogant and aloof.

Now pretend to be someone having a great day. They can handle anything coming their way; they can defend themselves if necessary, and they are looking out to see who they can befriend. Your chin should have risen just slightly above the horizontal for this one. You can see everyone and everything around you, boasting calmness, coolness, and confidence while making a good impression on others.

A neutral pose, where your chin is perfectly level and your eyes straight ahead is another good one, expressing purpose and confidence without any hint of arrogance or entitlement.

The further your chin goes down, the sadder and less confident you appear to people looking at you. Now, there is nothing wrong with feeling emotions, but do be careful not to express emotions that are not genuine, or that you don't especially want to advertise to others.

If you are a habitual sloucher, it can be hard to change your habits, but it's perfectly possible. Many of us today, children and adults alike, all suffer from something called "Forward Head Posture" caused by spending so much time crouching over our devices. When you have forced your spine into a position for so long, the body begins to automatically assume that position, and it neither looks nor feels very nice and is hard on your bones and joints. But it is fixable.

It's important to understand what it feels like when you're showing good posture. Here's how to tell if you're standing straight: stand with your back to a wall and then slowly shuffle backward until just your bottom and shoulders are touching the wall. (Don't cram your whole back up against the wall since you need to allow for the natural curve of your spine. You should be able to slip your hand between the small of your back and the wall). Next, raise your head until the back of your head is touching the wall. Draw yourself up tall as though a string is running from the top of your head to the ceiling. Your eyes should be naturally looking straight in front of you, with your ears over your shoulders and a straight line running down the length of your body from ear to shoulder to hip to knee to ankle. For most people, this is an example of good posture, and it's your target to be able to stand and walk like this all the time. It can seem impossible at first, especially if you have very poor posture to start with, but be mindful and persist with maintaining this head-up, shoulders-back position as often as you can, and it will soon become second nature.

Have you ever been scolded for having your hands in your pockets? Do you feel awkward if you're not holding something in your hands? You are not alone. We live such busy lives these days that it can seem wasteful or lazy to not be doing something all the time, even if it's just messaging friends on our phones, or googling a nearby location. But it's good manners to devote 100 percent of your attention to the person to whom you are speaking.

If you're a habitual "hands-in-pockets" offender, start wearing clothes without pockets for a while. Pockets are an amazing invention and incredibly useful, but you should go without them just for a short time as you learn to position your hands and arms naturally without the sanctuary of a pocket for them to rely on. When you are walking, your arms should swing naturally in counterpoint to the movement of your legs. Watch yourself in a mirror or big window and see if your gait looks even with your arms and legs moving naturally in straight arcs. Your feet should roll back to front with each step, and the left-to-right axis should be flat. That is to say, you should not roll your feet inward or outward as you walk. Minor pronation issues (pigeon toes and duck feet) can be fixed on your own simply by focusing on the way you put your feet down, but if your issues are severe and persistent, you might need to visit a doctor or podiatrist for corrective treatment or orthopedic shoes.

When you're standing stationary talking to others, avoid certain gestures like putting your hands on your hips, (a body language sign for aggression), and crossing your arms that can be interpreted as unwelcoming or aloof. Instead, allow one hand to fall naturally to your side while the other can be held behind your back or resting over your tummy—not touching it but just in front of it. This hand should hover somewhere around the third button on a jacket or over the general area of your belly button. You can also have your hands clasped behind your back (but check yourself in the mirror in this pose to make sure it doesn't affect the line of your clothing or your posture too much), or with one hand over the other above your front. The latter position is useful if you're holding something like a small clutch or a book.

Getting in and out of cars can be awkward, especially for women and girls in shorter dresses and skirts. A good way to avoid any embarrassment is to smooth your skirt down (if you're wearing a skirt or a dress), sit on the car seat with your legs outside the vehicle, then lift your feet up and swivel them into the car. Make sure you keep your knees and ankles fairly close together, using the door to shield your modesty, if necessary. Practice this in advance as it can be a tricky maneuver to master in the heat of the moment—and try to adopt this as it's more forgiving on your hips and legs.

Getting out of the car is the same: use your hands to balance your body, draw your feet and ankles together, and swing them out and down in one flowing movement. Ensure your feet are firmly on the ground before attempting to stand.

Men or nonbinary/unisex people can step into the car with their near leg, but any step should be as small and modest as possible—no wide-legged leap into the car seat needed. Getting out of the car is similar: open the door as wide as necessary, place one foot on the ground, and ease the rest of your body out of the car and onto your foot, bringing the other out to join the first in a smooth movement.

When going in and out of buildings, you should always pay attention to your surroundings, particularly who is around you and in which direction they're moving. It is usually considered courteous to let those who are on their way out go first, and then those who are entering can make their move. This practice can also be applied to elevators, buses, taxis, and trains. It's simple to understand that it will be much easier to move around when the building, elevator, or vehicle has fewer people in it. While you don't have to let everyone go in front of you (this can sometimes leave you standing by a doorway for a long time as you wait politely for others to pile in), do make sure you're mindful of people who might be more vulnerable: the elderly, young children, especially if they've lagged behind their parents, anyone who is disabled or has mobility issues, or other circumstances that might mean they need a modicum of extra courtesy from those around them.

As you will see from this example, many of the rules of etiquette are little more than common sense and—as the old saying goes—a matter of treating others as you would like to be treated yourself.

On the street, men should naturally take a protective position between the women and the road, in order to ensure their safety over that of the man. However, adhering to this point of etiquette, and many others too, should never be insisted upon if it will cause more trouble than it is worth. Instead, simply wait until the chance arises to assume the "correct" position when possible.

    Traditionally, men should allow women to enter and exit elevators first unless doing so will cause inconvenience to them or other elevator users. The same applies to revolving doors, although most revolving doors are automatic, and the man is no longer expected to take on the chivalrous burden of pushing the door around twice.

> FUN FACT: *Early revolving door etiquette demanded that men enter the door space first followed by his wife, but she would leave the revolving door first, while he completed two revolutions before rejoining her. That way she would never have to push the door around by herself.*

Despite modern thought, staircase etiquette has remained the same: in all cases, the woman or superior (for example, a business executive or elder) should ascend the stairs first with the man or underling following a step or two behind. The mindset here is that should the woman or superior person stumble or trip, the man or underling will be able to catch them and prevent their fall. The same applies when coming down the stairs: the man or underling should lead the way by a step or two, again giving the other (of socially higher class) a buffer between them and a tumble down the stairs.

When you're dining formally, you should wait to be seated—slightly less formal events will have a seating chart so you can find your own place. For very formal occasions, the server or maître d' will lead you to your seat, pull out your chair, and, as you sit, smoothly tuck it in so you're the perfect distance from the table for both comfort and easy eating. At other formal events, a gentleman will usually hold a lady's chair for her (usually the lady to his right, especially if you're with strangers providing the same service) and then seat himself. If you do have to seat yourself, pull out the chair only as much as you need to, then lift the chair as you tuck yourself in—never scrape it along the ground in a series of jerks. We will have a more in-depth look at dining room behavior in the third section, which is all about food and how to eat gracefully.

When seated in regular chairs, such as in living rooms or in interviews, there are some poses to take that can provide you with the peace of mind of knowing that your modesty will be preserved. Here are a few:

- The Sideways Slant: notably used by Katherine, Princess of Wales, this pose involves having the legs tilt one way to the knees which are firmly held together, before tilting the other way from the knees to the feet. This zigzag seating style ensures that even the most aggressive paparazzo cannot catch a glimpse of thigh (or worse) and gives the legs an elegant look, (for ladies).

- The Daring Knee Cross: this slightly controversial pose, as ladies traditionally never crossed their legs at the knee, is similar to the Sideways Slant, albeit with the legs tightly crossed at the knee, and pressed together to the ankle and feet. If done correctly, it looks elegant and stylish, while allowing a hint of personality and flare, (for ladies).

- Crossed Ankles: the traditional way for a lady to cross her legs, this pose involves sitting straight with the legs to the knees together and straight, and the lower legs crossed just at the ankle for a modest yet comfortable position, (for ladies).

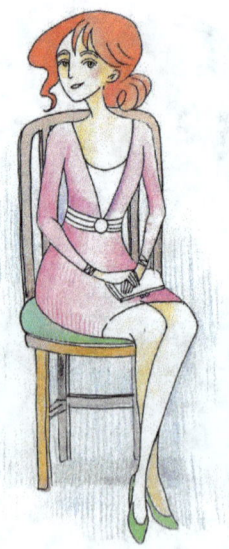

- Straight Sit-Up: with this pose you will simply have your legs form a right angle—thighs and knees together, right angle at the knee and feet running straight to the ground with feet and ankles neatly together, skirt or dress smoothed over the knees, (for ladies, but also suitable for men and nonbinary persons).

- Elegant Interest: this sitting position involves hooking an elbow over the back of your seat, so this pose can only be used in appropriate chairs or seats, while your legs are crossed at the knee, the whole body twisted slightly toward the person you're conversing with. This position looks elegant and is great for showing that you're being attentive and interested in the person you are speaking to. (This position is for men/nonbinary or unisex people—it would not be considered elegant for a lady to sit like this).

- Casual Conversationalist: sit comfortably in the chair, leaning forward a little to show you're paying attention, with your feet about shoulder-width apart (more than this is heading into "manspreading" territory, and it's rude and does not look at all attractive). Your arms can rest on the armrests, or you can rest your hands on your thighs or knees, or even gently clasp them in front of you. This is a lovely, relaxed style of sitting that supports good posture and looks good. (This is a suitable position for men and nonbinary).

FUN FACT: *Learning is a great way to improve yourself. For example, learning a new language not only helps you engage with people from other countries, but it also actually rewires and strengthens parts of your brain that are used in other areas of life. So, you can learn Japanese for fun and end up enriching your cognitive abilities and boosting your critical thinking skills at the same time. Win-win!*

- Defensive Pose: this is how NOT to sit. Leaning far back in your chair with your arms folded across your chest is a good way to let your conversation partner know that you're uncomfortable or uninterested in what they're saying, or that you disagree with them. Be mindful of your body language even when you're sitting down as you might be surprised to realize just how much people can discern your mood from the nuances of your posture.

SECTION THREE:
GETTING OUT THERE

Chapter four:
Nice to Meet You!

Okay, so now you're as clean and attractive as possible, well-dressed with appropriate footwear, and ready for the next part of your etiquette adventure.

The next step is meeting other people and doing it confidently and comfortably (for both of you).

Whatever the event you're attending, always go to the main entrance first: the front door, the hotel reception, or the restaurant lobby. Give your name clearly and then state the party you're joining, even at a private house. "Hello, I'm [name], and I'm here to attend [name's event]." (For example: "I'm Shelley and I'm here for Brandon's party"). By doing this, you're ensuring that there's no confusion as to who you are and why you're there. Usually, your host will be the one who opens the door at which point a handshake or a kiss (depending on your relationship) is appropriate. At other times, a third party will welcome you in and take you to the person who invited you—and again, this is the point when you offer a handshake or a kiss. We'll get into handshakes and kisses in just a moment, but first let's continue with introductions. Good hosts will always introduce you to as many people as possible. When this happens, look attentively at the person, note something distinctive about them, and repeat the name out loud.

"This is Tony." Tony has a ponytail and a tiny goatee. You say, "Hi, Tony," all the while imprinting the goatee and ponytail with the name in your mind.

This will help to anchor their name in your memory by association with their physical appearance. The next time you see the distinctive hair, the name "Tony" should float into your mind. But should you completely forget every name and distinguishing feature the moment you hear and see them, don't panic. It isn't poor etiquette to forget lots of new names all introduced to you at the same time. It would be a real feat of memory if you did remember everyone! Instead, when you come across someone to whom you were introduced and want to speak to, simply go up to them and say, "Hello again. Our host introduced us a moment ago. Please remind me of your name. I wanted to know more about the [fascinating thing you want to talk to them about]."

When shaking hands, make sure yours are clean and dry. You may not be able to do a lot about sweaty palms but rinsing them with cool water every so often and drying them thoroughly can help.

When a handshake is imminent (and you'll have to play this by ear as it will be slightly different each time, but usually wait for the introducer to say both of your names first), offer your hand with intent, but not too much force. Don't jab it out at them, but also don't force them to step closer to be able to reach your hand. Ideally, your hands should meet comfortably halfway between your bodies. Handshakes should be anything from one to three "shakes"—a pump up and back down to the starting position is one "shake"—before you release their hand again. It is incredibly awkward to continue holding someone's hand when they're trying to pull away, and it's very rude to use the handshake as some kind of muscle contest. Handshakes are polite, not tests of strength, but should also be firm and not floppy.

> PRO TIP: *If someone does ever squeeze your hand painfully in an effort to express dominance, let your hand go completely limp. By relaxing all the muscles and tendons in your hand, the squeeze will not hurt you as much as it would otherwise, so you can look politely puzzled at their rude and showy antics, rather than be left whimpering and cradling your wounded hand.*

Needless to say, when shaking hands neither party should use this contact to pull the other off balance—again, this is extremely rude and a breach of basic etiquette.

    If your host is overexcited and forgets to introduce you to anyone, you can introduce yourself. Smile politely, offer your hand to them, and say clearly, "Hi, I'm Shelley. I go to school with [host]. How do you two know each other?" They should respond with their names and an answer to your question, but if they do not, feel free to ask for their names in turn. "And what's your name?" is perfectly acceptable. Avoid using words like "sorry" and calling-out your host for their lack of propriety. Shame on you for berating and embarrassing the host in front of other guests, causing discomfort for everyone at the event.

    Occasionally, you will be the person who needs to make the introductions. Always start by saying something like, "Do you two know each other?" because if they are already acquainted, you'll feel pretty lame if you say, "Bob, this is Sid. Sid, this is Bob," only to have one or both of them say, "Oh, we know each other. In fact, we're cousins!" or something similar.

    When you're introducing yourself to others, use the name format they adopt. So, if your new acquaintance says, "Hello, I'm Bob Jones," you should respond similarly, offering a "hello" and your full name.

    "How do you do?" can be a confusing greeting. On the face of it, the person is asking how you're doing—or so it seems! In fact, the question is rhetorical, and you should respond with exactly the same in reply: "How do you do?"

    Phrases like, "Nice to meet you" and "Good to see you" are also conventionally polite, but they should be saved for after a conversation or period of chat. Coming too soon after meeting the person can make you sound insincere or obsequious.

> PRO TIP: *"More important" from an etiquette point of view can include, women over men, older people over younger ones, and in each case, you should name the "more important" person first out of deference. You are introducing the lesser person to them, thus: "Important" person, may I introduce the "Less" Important Person to you." You do not need to reverse this process. Introductions such as, "Bob, this is Sam. Sam, this is Bob," might seem correct and unbiased, but is actually poor etiquette.*

Avoid the use of nicknames when introducing people to each other. Allow the owner of the nickname to control who has privy to it. However, do try to temper your introduction with an interesting comment such as, "Mom, please let me introduce Natalie to you. Natalie has just returned from a two-week Parisienne vacation. Natalie, my mom studied in Paris in early 2014." This gives the new acquaintances something interesting to discuss (and a commonality) while they get to know each other.

And finally, make sure you pronounce names correctly—check beforehand. Sometimes this is as simple as asking the person, "What is the correct way to pronounce your name, please?"

Social kissing is very awkward, especially for younger people. In Europe, it's a common greeting with no gender differences regarding who kisses whom. In Italy, there can be up to two kisses, three are common in the Netherlands and France, so you would go right-left-right. Some countries go for full-contact kisses with the mouth contacting the recipient's cheek. However, in the US, when kisses are exchanged (and this is rare), it's a single "air kiss" blown in the ether, two or three inches away from the face, or perhaps touching cheeks. Sometimes these no-contact air kisses will come in pairs, again starting with the right side. But the handshake is much more common, and it's easy enough to politely dodge a social kiss if you're uncomfortable with such intimate contact with a near-stranger.

Following the COVID-19 outbreak of the early 2020s, social kissing and even handshakes were replaced with touchless greetings. These include the slightly awkward "elbow/fist bump," a prayer-like "namaste" motion, clasping both hands over your chest in a welcoming gesture, or nodding and expressing your welcome verbally, while keeping your hands firmly behind your back to let your guests or visitors know you're opting for a touchless greeting. Finally, there's the popular wave of the hand from a suitable distance instead of stepping into each other's personal bubble. It's acceptable to explain your desire for a touchless greeting: "I would love to shake your hand, but I have a cold and don't want to make you ill," or "I prefer contactless greetings, but please do come in and . . ." A good way to ensure this does not offend anyone is to stop short of the other person's proximity.

If they extend their hand to shake and are rebuffed in that position, they might feel hurt or snubbed.

Returning to introductions for a while, how do you act if you mishear a name when you're introduced? Of course, if you don't know that you've misheard it, there's not a lot you can do except pay attention when speaking to your new acquaintance. If anyone reacts to the way you say their name, stop, ask them if you're saying it correctly, and listen carefully to their reply. If you struggle to hear the person you're speaking to against the hubbub of chatter, don't be embarrassed to say so, and ask them to jot it down for you, or to step to a quieter part of the room. If you don't acknowledge the problem but persist in asking for their name, they may become very uncomfortable and begin to worry that they are the problem!

Making eye contact is a strange topic. It's a common belief that making constant eye contact is a sign of honesty and openness, but this is far from the truth. People think that a liar would be ashamed of their lies, and thus want to avoid eye contact, therefore anyone making bold eye contact must be an honest person. This is a fallacy. Eye contact is more often a sign of interest rather than honesty, and even then, people commonly glance around themselves, look for others, even examine their own toes (in or out of shoes), or the backs of their hands with long glances at the topic of their interest.

Staring intently at the person you're speaking to without blinking or looking away can actually begin to feel quite menacing, so be careful to glance around you, or look away from time to time, even as you respond to any questions or statements. As long as you maintain eye contact with the person you're conversing with for the majority of the time, they will feel flattered and certain that they're impressing you with their repartee.

But while maintaining reasonable eye contact is a good way to show the other person that you're listening and engaged, make sure your body language and facial expressions are in sync with your manners. A pinched, closed mouth and narrow eyes can make it appear that you're mistrustful or skeptical, while wide eyes and a softer mouth indicate interest and engagement.

Giving compliments is another minefield for young adults and teens. Childhood, with its absolute embargo on lying, is not so very far behind when you're thrust into situations where telling the truth would be rude. For example, if someone has a hideous haircut or piece of jewelry and they ask for your opinion on it, you genuinely cannot think of anything nice to say about it, but you must respond with something positive – what are you to do? Really, would a little white lie harm anyone?

The game plan – be mildly deceptive without uttering a single falsehood.

> FUN FACT: *A famous actor was often asked for his opinion on new and young actors. He never wanted to crush their dreams and ambitions by being brutally honest, so instead he would dress up his answers in such a way that they seemed to be complimentary, while in fact they were actually the opposite. One typical statement delivered with a huge smile was: "Darling! What a performance! Magnificent is not the word!"*

While you don't have to go quite as far as this actor, you can use words like "interesting" or "intriguing" in place of "lovely" or "beautiful"—or you can be honest in saying something like, "It's not my personal favorite, but I can see the excellent craftsmanship." There is almost always something to praise if you delve deeply.

Receiving compliments can feel awkward if you're not accustomed to them, but try not to respond to comments like, "You look lovely tonight" with deprecating comments like, "Oh, this old thing?" or "I think it makes me look fat." (Even if you think that's true). Instead, learn to accept compliments graciously: "You look lovely tonight." "Thank you so much." Don't hurry to return their compliment as this can seem insincere; wait for the right moment and give a genuine compliment back.

Moving onto gifts that you might receive, and those you might give in certain circumstances. Gift giving should be a joyous event—the act of giving people things that make them happy and receiving gifts that make you happy.

However, this simple exchange can give rise to misunderstanding and upsets if one party doesn't grasp the unwritten rules of gift giving. When you're invited to dinner at someone's house, it's always polite and appropriate to ask if you can bring anything with you. If the offer is declined, you can still bring a small gift: something nice, low-key, but still thoughtful—a box of delicious cookies or a bouquet of flowers. Once again, this depends on how well you know the person you're visiting and whether they'll feel comfortable with you spending time and money on them. If you're a plus-one, there's no obligation on you at all, but you might want to persuade the invitee (the person who is bringing you as their plus-one) to buy something for your hosts, a gift that can be from both of you or just from the invitee.

When you're given a gift that seems inappropriate, there are two ways to respond. The first is to decline too generous a gift. "Thank you so much, but this is too expensive a gift. I cannot accept it at this time, but I very much appreciate the thought." The second way, when given a gift that seems inappropriate, poorly conceived, and generally tacky or underwhelming is to smile (as genuine a smile as you can muster), thank the gift giver sincerely, assure them that you adore it and will put it to good use. Then, make sure you take the gift home with you, even if you hide it in a storage box, never to be seen again! Leaving a gift behind is unnecessarily rude to the gift giver who will be hurt and possibly even angered by your ungracious behavior.

When you're speaking to people you don't know, or at least don't know well, be careful to create a good impression. It's all too easy to nervously chatter about anything and everything under the sun, sometimes even circling back and beginning to repeat yourself because you don't want to go the other way and stand there in awkward silence with both of you waiting for the other to speak first.

Instead, think of your side of the conversation as part of a partnership. Make an overture and introduce (or reintroduce) yourself, then ask them something neutral, such as, details about the event you're attending.

"This is a lovely room. Have you been to many of these charity fundraisers?"

Use appropriate language. A good tip is to read luxury brand advertisements and see what adjectives and adverbs they use. Make a note of some of these and introduce them into your everyday vernacular. This will help to ensure you don't spend a whole conversation saying your mantra that things are "really nice" when you could be saying that you find them "exquisite," "gorgeously opulent," "deliciously piquant," and so on.

Having made your overture, wait for them to reply. In some conversations you'll feel as though you're the only one trying to be polite—and etiquette has your back here too. After two or three attempts to get a conversational ball rolling, you are well within your rights to smile and say, "Lovely to meet you, I'm just going to catch up with some people before they head off," or something similar.

Other alternatives are to point vaguely and say, "Excuse me, I'll just . . ." and wander off to find someone who looks more amenable to conversation. Or, "I think I see my friend, so nice to chat." This can be a little white lie; a minor deception is much preferable to saying, "Well, you're really boring, thanks for making the effort to chat!" and stomping off in a sarcastic huff. These sorts of polite untruths are tricky ground, but they can stand you in good stead when you're not very sure of your position in any particular group, and they can give you an easy out when you're faced with rude or condescending behavior.

If they do respond to your attempts to spark a conversation, make sure you listen carefully to what they say so you can reply meaningfully. A surprising number of people do not listen to those they're conversing with, instead merely waiting impatiently to have their turn to talk again— just wanting to hear their own voice saying fascinating things. While they're talking, as you focus on them, respond as they speak: little laughs at appropriate moments, nods of understanding or appreciation, even little sounds like "mmm," or "uh-huh." These sounds are called "response tokens" and they refer to nonverbal conversational contributions. The purpose of these sounds is to reassure your conversation partner that you are, indeed, actively listening to them and fully engaged. Allow yourself to react in these natural ways to conversation; they can help you focus on what's being said.

If you find yourself disagreeing with something they're saying, it's best not to be confrontational. If the issue is an important one, you can say something noncommittal that lets them know that you respectfully disagree. Practice saying little phrases that you can deploy at these moments: "That's not been my experience with [whatever], I'm surprised" or "That's a strong opinion . . ." In this way, you're letting them know that this conversation is not one you wish to pursue any further, but you'll have done so without (hopefully!) offending them or causing any awkwardness.

Always avoid overt claims that they're wrong, as this can be uncomfortable for everyone and leave them with the impression that you're hotheaded and rude. If the other person's comments or behaviors are egregious, then you can let your host know later that you did not appreciate their behavior and that you'd prefer not to be in their company in the future, if it can be avoided at all.

> FUN FACT: *Terry Pratchett's Discworld features two aristocratic families in a perpetual feud over the span of several years that they've agreed to only speak in absolute truths to one another, so there is no possible chance of an argument ensuing, saying things like:*
>
> *"The rain was very wet this morning, as always."*
> *"Indeed. Rain is customarily wet."*
>
> *"Quite right."*

> *And so on. Of course, Pratchett wrote humorous books, but this is a satirical commentary on how some real feuds were handled in polite society!*

Your choice of words is important too; selecting the right vocabulary and tone of voice can carry your charm and appeal to your audience. It's a fact that the most intelligent and interesting people tend to talk little and fairly quietly, actively listening much more than they speak. On the other hand, a pompous pontificator rambling on with great verbosity tends to become tedious. (That is to say, talking a lot and using fancy words soon gets boring!) Always use the simplest words to express interesting ideas, rather than merely spouting out a parcel of big words—and if in doubt, keep your mouth shut, your ears open, and let others educate you. That's why we have two ears, and only one mouth.

As a rule, avoid profanity and all but the most harmless jokes. Even if others are being something of a potty mouth or telling jokes that are edgy, irreverent, or slightly rude, you should refrain, especially if you're new to the group.

Forgotten the name of the person you were speaking to? No problem at all, simply lean in and say, "I'm so sorry, I didn't catch your name," and when they repeat it, say it to yourself four or five times, out loud (it really does help you remember it). If you still didn't catch their name, say, "And how do you spell that?" (Hoping, of course, that they don't look you in the eye and say, "S-A-M"). Always blame yourself for not hearing them clearly, "I'm so sorry, I'm a little deaf this evening," even if they mumbled. Finally, make sure you speak clearly yourself, even if you're shy. There's little worse than being taken to task for mumbling when you already wish the world would open up and swallow you.

Once you've arrived at the event successfully greeted your host and been introduced (or introduced yourself) to one or two people, you should venture deeper into the event going solo. Your host, even if they're the only person you know, will be far too busy coordinating the event, making time to greet every single guest, and making sure the hors d'oeuvres are laid out on time and that the soft drinks keep flowing. They won't have time to hold your hand and accompany you around the whole venue. Get a drink, or perhaps a plate with a few appetizers on it, and move slowly and steadily, checking out people's faces and body language. If you see someone looking awkward and out of place, that is your entrée: pause by them, make a neutral conversational gambit, and wait to see if it's reciprocated. Small talk is often decried as a waste of time, and it can be—but it's also a lovely way to make sure that conversations begin. They can always get more serious once you've gotten to know each other a little.

"Lovely room, isn't it?"
"How do you know [Host]? I go to school with them."
"Do you know when the speeches will begin?"

If you don't see people by themselves, you may have to try and insert yourself into a group, which can be very awkward, unless the clique is practicing good etiquette, in which case they'll make you welcome. In any case, you can offer a few conversational starters and responses and then smoothly move on, until you've acknowledged, greeted, or met most of the other guests. At this point, you can return to people you know, or find a good bird's-eye view from which to observe the event.

Whatever you're doing, keep an eye out for people who might need some assistance: hold a coat for someone to put on or take off, for example. Simply step forward with a murmur of "Allow me," perform the action, and then step back. Standing too close to anyone is uncomfortable. If you step forward to offer help and you're told, "No, thank you," step back and return to what you were doing—insisting on helping someone who has declined your offer is just as bad as watching them struggle.

Keep a little notebook (or file on your computer, or memo in your phone—whichever works best for you) in which you detail good ideas for conversation starters, mild anecdotes, or amusing or entertaining ways to introduce yourself. And practice these in the run-up to the event. It's so hard to remember witticisms when you're in an unfamiliar environment, surrounded by strangers, and feeling desperate to remember that perfect one-liner you know you had memorized earlier that day.

Whenever you're conversing with strangers take a cue from their expressions and body language, and if they begin to seem offish or unwelcoming, simply move on as quickly as you reasonably can.

You have arrived, greeted your host, and met a lot of people, making polite conversation and doing some excellent networking. But now it's dinnertime.

SECTION FOUR:
LET'S EAT AND BE MERRY!

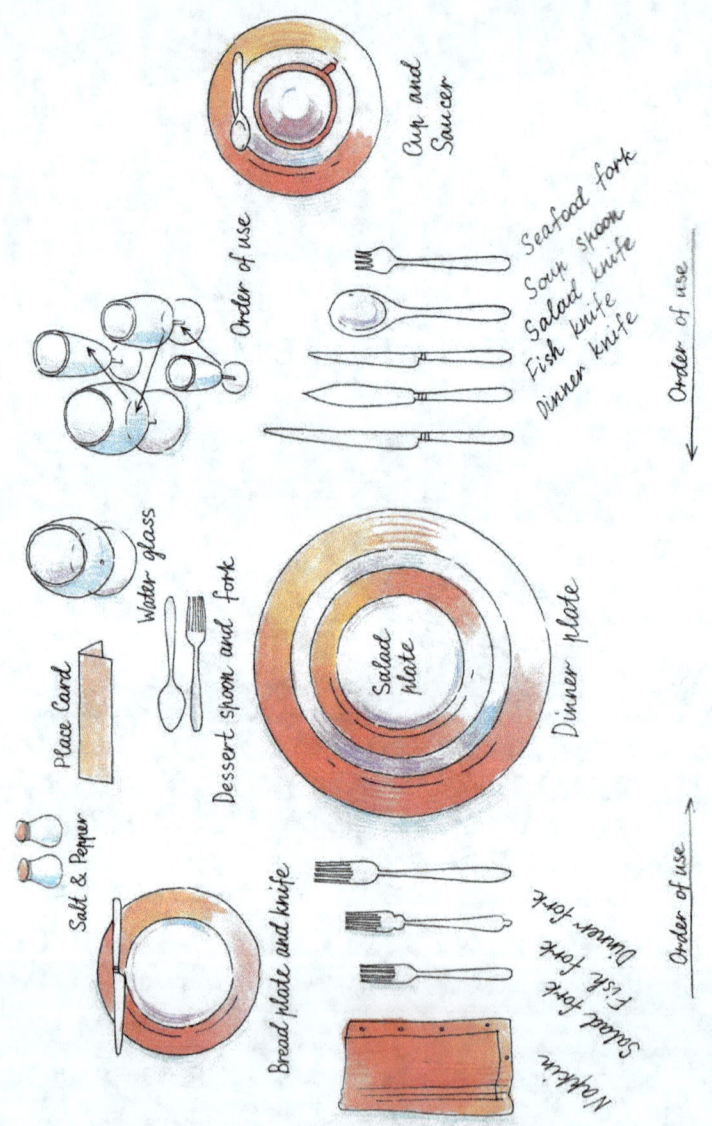

Chapter five:
Table Settings

It's something of a common trope in movies and television: a poor person is brought into a fancy dinner and struggles to make sense of the array of knives, forks, and spoons laid out in front of them—and that's before we even look at the various plates and bowls and glasses (water glass, wine glass, dessert wine glass, tumbler, highball) that you might come across. While the basic rule is to start on the outside and work your way in, let's take a look at the various items you might find on the table:

As you can see from this detailed and somewhat complicated image, there might be a lot of stuff on the dining table. And with so much stuff there, it can be easy to forget which spoon is for soup, or which knife you should use to butter your bread roll. But take a deep breath, check what others are doing, and remember that the entire system of etiquette is designed to make you feel at ease. If you do not feel at ease, then that is not your fault--something has gone wrong with the system, not you!

American / Continental table setting

The first time you eat at a fancy restaurant with multiple courses you might feel a little intimidated, but pretty soon you'll get the hang of it and be able to discreetly help other newcomers assimilate to the fine dining life.

Other countries use slightly different table settings than the United States, but the same rules tend to apply, except in restaurants where you're supplied with the relevant cutlery and glasses along with the food. This makes it easier for service personnel to make sure that someone ordering a steak has a steak knife supplied to them.

French table setting

Chapter six:
Service

In the event of a full-service dinner, you should not have to do anything for yourself, except perhaps pour your own water, if there's a water pitcher on the table. But expect to be guided into your seat, tucked in, and even have your serviette or napkin placed on your lap. Depending on the meal, servers will either take individual orders or they will circulate the table, offering you a choice of many dishes, which you can choose to accept or decline. Your drink (except for water, as mentioned above) should be kept topped off for you, and if your glass is empty, you can indicate you would like a refill with a discreet signal to the nearest server who should promptly remedy the issue.

The less formal the event, the less the servers will be involved, and you will be left to seat yourselves even if they show you to the table. The most informal places could have you go to the till to place your order, or it might even be a buffet where you and all the other attendees line up to help yourselves from the many chafing dishes and bains-marie set up on the food tables. With self-service events, keep your portion sizes modest and avoid filling up your plate. It is also an absolute no-no to take a large amount from any one dish; instead take a few spoonfuls (or equivalent), and return to your table to enjoy those before returning for more, if you are still hungry and there's still food left. Overtly displaying hoggish behavior is extremely rude, so try to avoid this, even if you're famished.

If you're at a private dinner and all the food is on the dining table with everyone sitting around waiting to serve themselves, in general, take your cue from your host or hostess. While vegetables and side dishes will be on the table for you to help yourself, it's customary to wait for the host or hostess to hand plates to everyone (with or without carved meat or similar foods on them) before anyone starts helping themselves. Firstly, this is because you will not usually have your plate yet, but it also gives the hostess the chance to be in control of the meal for a brief moment and make any announcements or toasts before everyone gets engrossed in the food. If the hosts are religious, there may be a moment of prayer or grace too, when it's polite for you to drop your head and clasp your hands, even if you personally are a nonbeliever.

Once the side dishes begin to circulate, you can take spoonfuls as the bowls travel around the table. Always use the serving utensil to place the food on your plate, and then return it to the bowl before passing it up or down the table (in the US, dishes customarily circulate to the right, in the UK to the left, but in general, keep things moving in the same direction that they were traveling when they arrived to you).

If you have not yet received a dish and it seems to have come to rest a distance away from you, speak clearly but softly, asking for it to come your way. Usually, "Please pass the [whatever]" is sufficient, but if there's lively conversation, you might need to attract someone's attention first—so do pay attention to the placenames if you can see them.

Place each item on your plate separately—do not pile everything in a mound—and once again, be light-handed and take just a little from each platter, especially if there are a lot of different dishes, or if you know there are going to be multiple courses.

However, before you've placed a single thing on your plate, you should, as soon as the plate is placed in front of you, touch a cautious finger to the edge of the plate closest to you. This will let you know if the plate has been warmed and how hot it is exactly, so you'll be able to lift and hold your plate without dropping it, burning yourself, or otherwise embarrassing yourself or your host.

Quite often, as you are eating, you'll be left with inedible parts—shells, bones, pits, etc.—and deciding what to do with them can be a dilemma if you're not acquainted with the finer points of etiquette. It may surprise you to learn that discreetly taking fish bones out of your mouth by fork, or gently placing olive pits into your palm before placing them on the side of your plate is perfectly good manners. This applies to anything you cannot realistically be expected to eat as long as you're discreet about removing it from your mouth, preferably by the same way the food was delivered to the mouth. Food eaten from a fork should be removed with a fork, food eaten with the hands can be removed with your fingers—but always discreetly. Once you've mastered this, you are at liberty to place these items on the side of your plate, well away from the food you're still eating. They should be placed at eleven o'clock on your plate, toward the top and slightly to the left where they're out of the way from the rest of your food.

Condiments and sauces should be added using the included spoon or other delivery method (it could even be a squirt bottle) with judicious care. Leaving huge puddles of sauces or sprinkles of pepper on your plate is rather rude, letting others know that you have little in the way of judgment when it comes to sauces, and that you don't care if others, further around the table, miss out. It's infinitely better to take a little and come back for more later, rather than take too much and look piggish.

At a formal dinner, it can be intimidating seeing people making subtle hand gestures—or even not seeming to indicate in any way—only to have the waiting staff swoop in to take their empty plates, bring new dishes, or refill their drinks. Don't worry, there's no telepathy at play here. The servers are highly trained, and the diners are signaling their intentions and desires by using something called "silent service signals." The best known of these is to place your knife and fork together, aligned at "12 to 6" in the UK as a way of indicating that you're done eating and that this plate can be removed. The knife and fork can be placed at an angle too, say "11 to 5," in the USA, but this angle should not be extreme. For example, placing your cutlery pointing toward yourself or at right angles to your chair will raise eyebrows and possibly confuse the server. (Remember etiquette is not only for those who use it, it is also for those who facilitate events, such as servers and caterers). If you have stopped eating temporarily due to anything that causes you to leave the table (more on that below)—say you've excused yourself for a moment, or a phone call has come in—but you intend to return and continue eating, you should place your knife and fork diagonally on the plate, at angles to each other so they make a triangle (see illustrations for more detail).

Returning for a moment to when it's appropriate for you to leave the table: it is rarely appropriate to do this in the middle of a formal dinner, so do keep these interruptions to a minimum. Having said that, it happens sometimes, and as always, etiquette is in place to make sure this is as minimally disruptive as possible to all concerned.

You may need the bathroom quite urgently. Nervousness can wreak havoc on our bodies, after all. In this case, it must be stressed, do not wait until the last possible moment to relieve yourself. For gentlemen, it's a little easier as you can just push back your chair and murmur, "Excuse me for a moment," before hastening off. If a lady begins to rise, it's customary for the gentlemen sitting on her left (there will usually be one on either side) to help her to do so, by easing her chair out so she can rise without having to push the chair back herself. (If you're a man, you should be most attentive to the person seated to your right). This dates back to the days of voluminous skirts when women would frequently stand on their own skirts, or find that their chair legs were pinning the long dress in place, but the gesture has stood the test of time. In this case, assuming the gentleman moves to assist her, she should wait for him to begin to move the chair before standing by herself. Do not be alarmed if all the men at the table stand when you do; again, it's a customary practice for gentlemen to stand politely when a woman rises. Often, she'll say something like, "No, no, please stay seated," but this is often ignored as mere convention not actual instruction, and the men remain standing until the woman is out of the room, or a suitable distance away, if the room is a large one. The same will happen when she returns: the men will stand, and the man seated to her right (or a handy server) will help her back into her seat, tucking her into the table to resume her meal.

PRO TIP: *Never ask anyone where they are going when you see them leaving the table.*

Serviettes can be something of a minefield—even the name of them! In some cultures, the word "napkin" means diaper, while in many others "napkin" (as in serviette) is considered common, and "serviette" is used instead. Other cultures (for example, the British aristocracy, who delight in being contrary about these things) find "serviette" to be pretentious and stick with "napkin." Never tuck your serviette (or whatever you wish to call it) into your shirt front, no matter how messy you fear the meal will be, or how precious your dress—it is just not done. Instead, take your serviette and unfold it (they will sometimes be formed into textile sculptures, at other times merely folded once or twice), placing it on your lap. If you're wearing silky fabric, this can be a problem as serviettes can slide off your lap, so you may need to work to keep it in place. In some establishments, the server will place your serviette on your lap for you—don't be alarmed if this happens. Just act naturally and allow them to do their work. Serviettes can also be used in silent service signals, with a finished meal indicated by the placement of your serviette on the table by the left side of the plate, never on the plate itself. If you're returning to continue eating, place your serviette on your seat while you are absent.

During any meal, it's common to have pauses in the eating. These can be between courses, during speeches and toasts, or simply to enjoy the meal and the conversation. When this happens, it can be awkward when it comes to your hands. What should you do with them? If your fork has food on it, you can eat that mouthful while you listen to the other person, or you can simply place your loaded fork down on your plate, in the "I'm not finished" position as described above. You can rest your wrists on the edge of the table near the knife and fork, or you can place them in your lap. In Europe, the former is the most common placement, but in the US and UK, keeping your hands in your lap when not actively eating is the recommended stance. In general, keep your elbows off the table, but resting your wrists or a small portion of your forearm on the table is acceptable. Always be mindful of your table companions and avoid wild arm gestures and sweeping movements of your hands, especially near drinking glasses and other people's food, and keep your elbows down by your side. Elbows should never be placed on the table.

Serviettes are there to protect your clothes from food spills and they can also be used to dab—never rub—your mouth to make sure you don't have any lingering crumbs or gravy droplets clinging to your lips. You should never need to use them to clean your fingers, except for the smallest blob or splash of sauce or gravy. Finger foods—anything that is eaten with the hands—should automatically come with a finger bowl.

These are saucer-sized bowls with upright sides, and about an inch and a half or so deep. They're usually brought to the person with the finger food and placed at the top left of their place setting. More often than not, the water in the finger bowl is cool and has a slice of lemon or lime floating in it. Once you've finished the food, which could be anything from chicken wings to raw fruit to lobster claws, you should only need to dab your fingertips in the bowl of lemony water. The citrus oil in the peel and the acid in the juice should have infused the water enough for the lightest contact to dissolve the fat and grease from the food, leaving clean fingers which can then be patted dry on the serviette. Do not touch the floating slice in the bowl. It is neither for eating, nor to be used as a scourer on a particularly stubborn piece of food. In general, if you don't have a finger bowl, you're expected to use the silverware provided.

Chopsticks are often a source of embarrassment for Western diners who find themselves in Asian restaurants.

Here is a very quick list of dos and don'ts for you to remember:

- Do learn to hold them properly. They won't be as easy as a knife and fork, unless you've been using them since childhood, but still try your best.

- Don't stab your food with the tip of a chopstick. Food is symbolic of life and stabbing it is considered to be unlucky and crude.

- Do use a chopstick rest. This is a small stand that will be next to your plate. Place your chopsticks on this with the food end on the rest to keep it off the tablecloth.

- Don't point with your chopsticks. This is very disrespectful and rude—just as it would be if you did it with your knife and fork.

- Do share food with others by recommending morsels to them. However, if you're serving from a dish that you particularly like, pick up the piece with serving chopsticks and transfer it directly to their plate, or if they're providing you with the treat, allow them to place it on your plate. Transferring food from one set of chopsticks to another is reminiscent of Japanese death rituals and is taboo at meals.

- Don't rub your chopsticks together no matter how satisfying you find it, or how often you've seen other people do it. This is because it's done to remove splinters from cheap or poor-quality chopsticks and doing it in front of your hosts is tantamount to saying that you suspect them of providing you with shoddy eating utensils.

- Do decide what you would like first before picking up your chopsticks. Scan the table and pick one or two items to try, then pick up your set or the serving chopsticks, and help yourself—or others—to the food. When there are specific serving utensils you should use those.

- Don't stress too much! As long as you are honestly trying your best with these unfamiliar utensils and it can be seen that you're not a rude or uncouth person, any minor faux pas will be overlooked, or kindly and gently corrected.

> PRO TIP: *Practice using your chopsticks on larger pieces of food until your dexterity is mastered, and then go smaller until you can safely manage rice grains.*

If you're fortunate enough to be invited to an Eastern meal, you might find the place settings to be unfamiliar. Here's a quick overview of what to expect.

No matter what situation you find yourself in, and no matter how well prepared you are, there is always the chance you might stumble upon an unpredictable circumstance where you feel awkward and unsure of what to do. Here are some basic, common-sense ways you can react to stand you in good stead no matter what kind of situation you find yourself tackling.

If someone is upset, messy, or otherwise discombobulated take steps to minimize their exposure. Move to block others' view of them, discreetly offer help (and perhaps let them know what has happened). Keep your voice low and mute your movements so as not to draw attention to the crisis. If others have already gone to their rescue, refrain from staring, craning your neck to try and see what's going on, or speculating about what has happened to your table companions. Offer help if you think you can be useful, but do return to your seat if your offer is declined; think about how you would feel if your trousers split open, someone spilled their food or drink on you, or you began to have a minor medical issue in public. You wouldn't want people crowding around, pointing, or laughing—so don't do these things to others. Fortunately, moments like this are fairly rare, so they should not occur too often as you journey through the world of etiquette.

To return to the dining table, do not assume you can surround your place setting with personal belongings. When the food is brought out, along with drinks, water pitchers, finger bowls, and potentially even more cutlery, any "free" space will soon be occupied. Anything you bring with you should be tucked away into a clutch, handbag, or even into your pockets. Phones, sunglasses, or items like tissues and face masks should all be kept off the table.

Handbags should not be put on the table either. Most bags, even small clutch purses, often have a narrow strap which you can use to hang on the back of your chair.

Chapter seven:
Food, Glorious (Formal) Food

At last, we come to the things that are actually on your plate. At many formal meals the table will have a basket of bread in the center. These can be dinner rolls, breadsticks, slices of garlic bread, or even tender dough balls with a variety of accompanying dips. While you are absolutely meant to eat these, you should avoid stuffing yourself silly; it can be tempting, especially when you're nervous, feeling awkward, or are suddenly ravenous (having been too busy getting ready during the day to eat much), to gorge on the bread. Instead, take calming breaths, have a sip or two of water, and concentrate on listening to the head of the table if you are all around one big table, or have a go at making conversation with the people on your left or right, or across the table from you. You can open the conversation by offering the bread around before you take one slice, stick, or roll. Once you've done so, eat it slowly, chewing thoroughly, and swallowing small bites before attempting the next.

Starters or appetizers tend to be smallish plates containing light bites to stimulate the appetite for the main course. Often, for formal meals, this is soup. Use your round soup spoon and scoop it away from you, toward the far side of your bowl. You should sit upright, leaning forward just enough that your mouth is over your bowl. This will mean that any accidental soup spills will go back into the bowl rather than dribble on the tablecloth or down your front. Soup is always spoken of as being "drunk," by the way, never "eaten," even though the action feels more like eating than drinking. (NB: Do not *literally* drink your soup, and certainly don't slurp it).

Other starters can be shared platters. You will almost always have a small plate to serve yourself from the shared platter. Again, bear in mind how many other people are sharing the dish with you before you get dibs on it. With multicourse meals, always eat modest portions to leave room for the other courses—they are often worth it. (And that's another reason for avoiding the bread or strictly limiting your portion size).

The main course is called the entrée in the USA.

> FUN FACT: *In old French menus, the starter or appetizer was followed by hors d'oeuvres, which was then followed by a course called the entrée. The main course, most often a meat roast, followed this, and then sweet endings with dessert and/or cheese plates. As very few people could afford to have these lavish five- or six-course meals, they were slowly whittled down to three- or four-course meals with Europe merging the first two or three courses to adopt "entrée" as an alternative word for "starter," while the USA transformed "entrée" to mean the course after the starter—the main course.*

Other single dishes will be served to you, some coming with specialist cutlery to use (melons, for example, require a delicate spoon with a serrated edge to cut through the flesh, sweet baked treats are accompanied by a cake fork designed with three curved tines for graceful indulgence, and ice cream sundaes will come with a long spoon that can reach the bottom of the glass in which the treat is served). Otherwise, revert to the tried and trusted method of using cutlery from the outside in.

Any meal, no matter how formal, can leave you with something inedible parked in your mouth that you would really rather not have in there. This can be anything from fruit pits to fish bones to unchewable pieces of gristle that were embedded in your otherwise perfect steak, and as mentioned earlier, in most cases, you can remove these things discreetly from your mouth as required.

    This also applies when there's something unpleasant in your food that shouldn't be there—a hair, for example, or something that doesn't belong in your meal. Remove it discreetly, and when you can attract the attention of a server or attendant point out the problem in a neutral manner with a quiet voice. Just because your meal has been marred, it's no reason to disturb the other diners whose meals are most likely all fine. Food that is inedible because it's very badly overcooked or undercooked can be sent back. Once again, use your discretion so as not to embarrass your host or disturb other diners. State the problem simply and let the server know how they can best remedy it for you: "My chicken is raw. Please, can it be properly cooked," or, "Please cook me a new piece of chicken, ensuring it is thoroughly cooked this time."

> PRO TIP: *While red meat in solid cuts (e.g., steak, roast beef, etc.) can be enjoyed rare and is usually safe to eat despite only being lightly cooked, ground beef (such as that found in burgers) and white meats such as pork and chicken, should always be thoroughly cooked to ensure that harmful bacteria are destroyed.*

Toothpicks should be used if needed (they're often on the table in a small pot, individually wrapped) to remove chunks of food that are lodged in your teeth. It's better to make discreet use of a toothpick for a few seconds (and that means leaving the table to do so in private, not doing it at the table) than to spend ages sucking your teeth trying to correct the issue without help. Older diners might need these more than young folk whose teeth are still in great condition and not loosened with age, but it's good to be aware of these things just in case you do end up with a piece of your dinner wedged immovably in your teeth.

Condiments and sauces might look different from how you're accustomed to seeing them: ketchup in bowls, for example, and mustard in mustard pots complete with tiny spoons. While these items are there to enhance the enjoyment of your meal, use them sparingly as food cooked by highly trained chefs will have a unique flavor that might be overwhelmed or drowned by piquant sauces. Traditionally, these are put onto the plate in the five o'clock position, and used from there as needed. The same frugality of use applies to salt and pepper; most chefs add sufficient seasoning that their food tastes best exactly as served needing no other "improvement." Even meals served with condiments that enhance the taste and texture (mint sauce with lamb or mutton, for example, applesauce with pork, and of course, cranberry sauce with turkey) should be subject to caution. Use sparingly, allowing the rest of your table companions to share the jar or pot. You can always get a little extra should you run out after everyone else has suitably adorned their meals.

The following list details various foods and how to eat them in a formal setting. However, some of them can also be served at more informal meals, which are covered in the next chapter. This will be noted if this is the case.

- Apples and pears: in formal settings, these should be eaten with the appropriate cutlery. The basic approach is to cut the fruit into quarters, slice out the seed core, and eat the remaining flesh with the dessert cutlery. In picnic settings, these can usually be eaten either whole, in hand, or from a plate, cut into slices which are then placed in your mouth with the hand.

- Artichokes: peel the leaves off by hand and dip them into the accompanying sauce, leaving the leaf tips—the less fleshy part—on the side of your plate. Once the leaves are finished, choose a knife and fork to access the artichoke heart which is sometimes served as a standalone dish.

- Asparagus: as a side dish or appetizer, these are one of the few foods that are acceptably eaten by hand. As part of a meal, they should be eaten in the same way as your other vegetables, with tough stalks left at eleven o'clock on the plate.

- Bananas: yes, these are eaten with a knife and fork in formal settings. Slice the top and bottom off, unwrap the peel, then slice and eat the banana using your knife and fork. In informal settings, you can eat bananas by hand, although some prefer to break off chunks of banana with the hand, rather than bite pieces off.

- Bread items: surprisingly, at formal events, bread is broken rather than cut with a small piece being pulled off the main bread item and buttered before being popped in the mouth. Repeat this with each individual bite.

- Burgers: while these are rarely seen at formal events, when they do appear, they should be eaten with a knife and fork. If the burger is especially thick and tall, you can take off the top bun and eat it separately to the bottom bun and patty. Alternate bites of the top bun with bites of the bottom to ensure the whole burger is finished at the same time.

- Wedges of cheese: these should be allowed to retain the wedge shape. Take slices of cheese, not chunks of it.

- Grapes: small, sweet, delicious, and very good-looking on a platter, grapes should be eaten with care. A large bunch should come with grape scissors to allow guests to snip off smaller bunches for their own consumption. If scissors are not provided, snap off small bunches with your fingers and place them on a plate.

- Kebabs: skewered chunks of meat and vegetables are great at barbecues where you'll be excused for getting a little sauce on your chin. But at more formal events, hold the skewer with one hand while you use your fork to slide all the food off the skewer and onto your plate. Then eat it as usual with your knife and fork.

- Mussels and oysters: sometimes, these will arrive at the table already loosened from the shell. If they are not loosened for you, use a fork to ease the flesh off the shell, then use that same fork to pop the morsel in your mouth. Oysters can be consumed straight from the shell, tipping them into your mouth in a smooth movement.

- Pasta: pasta and knives should not be used in conjunction with each other (except to guide the piece to the fork or hold it still for skewering). Never cut pasta pieces; instead use your fork to stab them or twirl longer pasta into a neat, easily edible bundle.

- Pizza: perhaps the most egalitarian of all foodstuffs, pizza can be found everywhere from formal balls to wayside diners, and it is usually eaten the same way in all these places—with the hands. However, if the pizza is heavily laden or has "sloppy" toppings, choose to use a knife and fork to slice off small bites.

- Salad: salad leaves should be folded rather than cut. This dates back to an old history in which cutting through salad leaves was said to be insulting to the host, as though you were searching for poisons concealed in the food.

- Salt and pepper: as a rule, if it's not on the table, you shouldn't need to add it to your food, so don't ask for condiments at formal events. If they are there, salt should be formed into a small heap on the side of your plate with you dipping forkfuls of food into this pile as needed. The only exception to this is if the salt is in a mill. Then you can sprinkle it over your meal just as you do with pepper.

- Souffle: tricky to make, but very easy to eat, as long as you remember to use a fork for savory souffles, and a spoon for sweet ones.

- Spaghetti: usually eaten with just a fork, although you can use a knife to guide recalcitrant bits of food into place on the fork. What is less permitted is the American practice of whirling the spaghetti around in a spoon. Any authentic Italian connoisseur seeing you do this will raise an eyebrow and think you are a bit of a baby.

- Steak: eat with a fork and a steak knife, slicing off morsels of meat and dipping them into a little puddle of sauce, rather than smothering the steak with the sauce.

- Sushi: to correctly eat sushi, you need to master chopsticks. And when you're dipping your sushi piece into the soy dip, make sure you only dip the fish side. The rice will break apart if you dip the grain.

- Tomato sauce: this—and all sauces—should be used sparingly, and only if provided. Place a little puddle on your plate and dip your food into it as necessary.

- Toast: like bread, toast should be buttered and eaten in small bits, rather than the whole slice buttered (and other garnish added) all at once.

 Other points to remember include only serving yourself within the confines of the plate, leaving the rim untouched and clean. This is to help the servers neatly serve and clear without getting food debris and sauce stains on their gloves or bare hands.

 Another point, please leave your empty plate in its place setting after the meal. Don't push it away from you or stack it with other diners' plates. This is not helpful to the service staff and can leave messy stains on the tablecloth.

 And finally, bear in mind that anything that has touched your mouth should only touch your plate, never the table or anywhere else. This includes silverware, inedible bits of food (seeds, gristle, bones, etc.), and anything else. The only exception would be your serviette or napkin, which should never be placed onto your used plate.

Chapter eight:
Informal Meals

Moving away from formal dinners, it can be something of a trial to decide if a food should be eaten with a knife and fork, or if you should dig in with your fingers. Burgers, for example, and pizzas, as mentioned previously, are two contentious foods because they can be eaten with a knife and a fork but are more naturally eaten with the hands. When you're in such a semi-informal setting, take cues from your hosts; if they are happily eating with their hands, if cutlery has not been laid out, and if there are finger bowls and wipes on the table, take this as a signal to emulate them and pick up your burger or pizza slice in your hands.

> FUN FACT: *Cucumber sandwiches are a popular "posh" food because in the 1700s and 1800s cucumbers were tricky to grow, requiring the use of a cucumber frame (a little flat glass-covered box in which the cucumbers could grow without suffering from cold temperatures, even in summer), and often meant that the host or hostess was affluent with extensive grounds, a skilled gardener, and the time and leisure to grow such "exotic" delights.*

Finger sandwiches should also be eaten with your hands, but always from a small plate— not directly from the serving platter—even if this is a paper plate or party serviette. Shared food like chips, nuts, olives, cheese, and crackers, or anything that might be freely available at a picnic or birthday party should be transferred to a small plate or your hand rather than eaten directly from the communal bowl. Always be mindful of the sensibilities of others: no double-dipping, take the first item you touch (no scavenging to find the biggest or best one), and make sure your hands are clean before helping yourself. More likely, though, there will be plates handy so you can load up your small plate with the items you want to eat without having to "graze" directly from the table. And once you've taken some of the food, move away to allow others access to the food table and to minimize the risk of you coughing or speaking over the exposed offerings.

But not all informal meals are without expectation of cutlery use. For example, garden parties appear to be picnic-like, but no one will eat cake with their fingers. Instead, they will use a cake fork, a small, three-tined utensil with a thickened "blade" side which is ideal for slicing bite-sized chunks of cake from the slice you have on your side plate.

Confusingly, sandwiches are meant to be eaten with the fingers, perhaps because they are made to be small and thin, each one requiring no more than two bites to consume. The same applies to canapés, which should always be small enough to eat in one bite, making them an easy food for standing buffets where the need to hold your plate and your glass at the same time means you have to perform some very careful juggling, or enlist the help of a willing companion.

When you're helping yourself to food at these informal occasions, bear your good manners in mind at all times. Tea parties, picnics, and garden parties all tend to offer a wide range of delicious treats, such as cupcakes, ice cream, full-sized cakes, pies, pancakes, waffles, cheesecakes, various fruits, and patisseries—anything that allows the chef to show off the full range of their skills. When picking one of a plateful of small treats, take the one closest to you rather than hunting around on the plate for your preferred piece.

Ice cream can be a tricky food at a party—unlike when you were a child. At informal occasions, you may be offered an ice cream in a cone, which can be a minefield. Eat your ice cream reasonably quickly, taking small bites (avoid licking your ice cream in long strokes of your tongue— this can seem quite rude for anyone over the age of twelve), and taking care that it doesn't drip. If it's a hot day and many people are struggling with their ice creams, ask for a bowl into which you can tip your cone, then eat it tidily with a spoon, using the cone to "mop up" any excesses. At more formal occasions, your ice cream will come in the form of two or three scoops artfully arranged on a plate or in a bowl, and you will have a spoon that's designed for eating ice cream.

Pizza is also a tricky food, especially at parties where it's less formal and you might not have a table to rest your plate on. Take small bites of your pizza, and ensure the toppings are firmly attached rather than sliding off, leaving melted cheese and pepperoni stains on your shirt and chin.

Straws should be used with care too. Grasp the straw in the hand that is not holding the glass and guide it to your mouth. Waving your tongue around in an attempt to capture the straw is certainly off-putting. And blowing bubbles is even rude for a toddler.

In all these cases (of eating and drinking in company), you should take care not to make unpleasant noises when eating: chomping, slurping, and licking your lips noisily are all signs of poor eating habits and are considered rude. Practice eating quietly—perhaps even make a video of yourself eating and assess your consumption skills as objectively as you can, correcting anything that might be rude or problematic.

Chapter nine:
Chitchat

Initiating conversations at formal events can be both easy and difficult, and you will usually be expected to make and return conversational overtures with as many guests as possible. Many of the interpersonal skills mentioned in an earlier chapter can be applied here: introducing yourself, making neutral and polite conversation, and ensuring that your seating companions are not neglected. Move slowly but steadily around the room if it is a gala event, trying to greet or acknowledge as many of the other guests as possible. Be mindful of your body language, whether you are approaching someone or being approached. An open posture invites others to approach, while defensive positions (folded arms and unwelcoming expressions or turned away face) are likely to make your fellow guests feel awkward. Pace yourself when doing this so you don't fall into a sort of daze in which you're merely parroting words that no longer make any sense to you, and you stop processing the guest's replies. One of the politest things you can do is to actively listen with care to your conversational partner.

When you're seated at a table and taking pains to include both of your immediate neighbors in conversation, make sure not to chat with each one for longer than a few minutes—five to ten is plenty—as this can mean that the neighbor on the other side is sitting without any interaction occurring if their other table neighbor is neglectful. However, if you're not the host of the event do not stress about it too much as a good host will be paying attention to the whole room and will soon rescue anyone who seems to be neglected by their tablemates.

This advice is also applicable at parties, buffets, and other social gatherings where people can wander about freely. You are there to be sociable, so do make the effort. It will be awkward at first, but after one or two enjoyable interactions you might find yourself beginning to love being a social butterfly.

If you're reading this section thinking to yourself, "I would love to be able to talk to a perfect stranger! How on earth do I even start though?" then the next part of the book is just for you!

When you're making conversation with strangers, avoid any topics which can be deemed sensitive: politics and religion are big no-no's, especially if you have unconventional ideas about them. Open questions are an excellent way to make sure the person properly engages with you in a way that closed questions (those that can be answered with a simple one-word answer) do not. An example of an open question is one like: "So, what sports and hobbies do you partake in?" The person being asked this question has to actively answer and give information about their favorite pastimes. For example, "I play volleyball with my local club—we're in the running for the championship!" This makes it much easier to ask a follow-up question, and before you know it, you're having a lively conversation. On the other hand, a closed question could be, "So, do you play soccer?" The person being asked can simply say, "Yes" or "No," throwing the conversational ball back into your court immediately, so you must continue to do the "heavy lifting" in the chat.

Other ways to engage with strangers include telling innocuous but funny jokes, asking about their work or school, and whether they enjoy or follow any sports teams. Read up a little about these things so you can at least hold your own in conversation. Another ploy to try would be to plead ignorance and allow them to teach you about their particular interests.

Remember to introduce yourself before asking about the other person. This simple act opens a bond between you, which will make it harder for them to snub you if that is their M.O.

When talking with strangers, avoid standing too close to them as this can be very off-putting, especially for socially anxious people with issues about personal space. While you're talking with them, maintain a respectful (but not excessive) distance, watch their body language for cues about whether your conversation is welcome or not, and take their lead if they seem to want to end the conversation or move away from you. When you need (or want) to move on, try to introduce people, who are otherwise alone, to someone new, but don't make a big issue of it. If there's no one readily available simply say, "It was lovely to meet you," and make a polite exit.

Chapter ten:
Technology at the Table

There's a lot of chat about what constitutes good phone etiquette, but it all boils down to one simple rule: if you are in doubt, don't take it out!

Some restaurants these days, including some very fancy ones require ordering by phone, in which case, of course, your device should be used. But afterwards, it should be put away again into a pocket or bag, preferably on silent mode for the duration of the meal. Your cellular device is *persona non grata* at most events, both formal and informal.

Formal meals should not be "Insta-ed"—and certainly never without your host's approval. Many other meals, too, benefit from having phones away with everyone paying attention to the conversation and being mindfully present. It's very awkward to sit at a meal while everyone is engrossed in their phones. One wonders if there's any point in meeting up if you're going to be ignored in favor of the latest crisis on Twitter or Snapchat.

If you're expecting an urgent or important call, let people know beforehand. Keep the phone use and checking to a minimum, and when the call comes through excuse yourself from the table and go somewhere out of earshot where you won't be disturbing anyone. But it is much more mannerly to ensure you're not disturbed during your meal if you can at all help it by rescheduling the call to a more convenient time.

FUN FACT: *In medieval times when the entire household dined at one big table, the salt (of which there would have been only one salt cellar) was placed in the middle. If you were "above the salt," this meant you were an honored guest or family member, sitting on the side of the table closer to the host, while those "below the salt" tended to be lesser family members, workers, and those not quite as favored. The saying, "He/She is above the salt," now means someone honorable and sure to do the right thing–a real mover and shaker.*

SECTION FIVE:
GETTING INTO DATING

Chapter eleven:
How to Make the First Move

It's a difficult time to be a young person interested in dating other young people. Issues around consent and reciprocity can make it feel as though it's a crime to be interested in getting to know someone, and parents and older siblings can't help much as times were different when they were taking their first steps into the world of romance. So, how can you show that you're into someone without coming across as creepy or pushy?

The best way to start dating anyone is to become friends with them first. Join clubs and sports teams where your interests align and get to know them in a social context first. Please note: do not join a club simply to get to know someone. Insincerity is obvious to all of those around you, and for your crush to find out that someone has joined a club purely to interact with them is the very definition of creepy! An added bonus of getting to know your crush before committing to anything is that you'll be able to see if your admiration is warranted. Even the prettiest girls or most handsome guys lose their appeal if they turn out to be mean or unkind to others. But hopefully, they will stand the test of closer proximity and you can begin to make friends with them.

Once you have an idea of their personality and perhaps some of their likes and dislikes, you can begin to express a more intimate interest by inviting your crush for a coffee or to see a movie. If they're interested in return they will accept, and you should be able to take things from there. However, some people will not understand your interest, perhaps modestly thinking that someone like you would never want to spend time with them, or maybe simply misread your invitation as being a group thing and inviting everyone along. If you receive such a setback without a clear refusal, you can persist with your gentle pursuit. But if at any point you're told to back off, or asked to keep your distance a little more, you should listen—the days of "just try harder until they give in" are long gone and thank goodness for that!

Chapter twelve:
Breaking Up Is Hard to Do

Breakups are horrible--everyone agrees on that. But some breakups can be made even harder by poor behavior on the part of the couple, singly or together.

If someone breaks up with you, listen to what they have to say and try to understand it from their perspective. If, for example, they say that you always have to be right and that leaves them feeling wrong-footed and silly a lot of the time, do not agree that they're wrong and silly. This is why they're breaking up with you! Instead, acknowledge your fault: "I do like to be right all the time," then apologize for making them feel this way. "I'm sorry I made you feel bad. I didn't mean for that to happen. It was thoughtless of me." Avoid apologies that place the blame on the other person: "I'm sorry you feel that way," for example, is a terrible apology. You are basically saying that they are in the wrong and that it's their sensitivity causing the problem, rather than your behavior. It is, in other words, a non-apology.

After a painful break-up, it's natural to lash out in anger and spite when we're hurt. Restrain these feelings, even if you genuinely do feel wronged by your partner's actions, or even if you are being wronged—unfortunately, there are troublemakers who like to tell tales and try to interfere with the relationships of others. Always try to have a face-to-face conversation about the reasons for break-ups, just in case that's what has happened here. Remember that sharing intimate details about your relationship with others in a bid to get back at your former partner is at best a betrayal (and a sign that you deserve to be dumped), and at worst, illegal (getting into the slander/libel territory here).

Don't do anything that you'd be ashamed of in the eyes of your favorite adults, or that you'd hide from your future children. This is a good philosophy for your whole life, not just for dealing with heartache.

PRO TIP: *If you don't like your own company, why would anyone else want to spend time with you? This sounds a bit harsh, and it is, but it's also true. There are a great many young people who cling to relationships long after the romance has gone, or who switch from one partner to another within a very short time. These people cannot bear to be alone, romantically speaking, because they have no inner resources upon which to rely, and they become sad or depressed without a significant other to raise their spirits and give them a reason to get dressed in the morning. Learn to enjoy your own company and you'll find the quality of your relationships improve immeasurably when you're seeking out each other's company because you enjoy it, not because it fills a void inside.*

Chapter thirteen:
Gifts and Giving

You may be so deeply in love with your new boy- or girlfriend that you want to buy them everything they desire, no matter how much it costs, even though you've only been dating a short time. Hold back on emptying your savings account to get them the perfect expensive gift. Not only are very lavish presents in the early days of a relationship frowned upon from an etiquette perspective, but it can, on a purely practical level, turn out to be a very poor investment. What if they take your extravagant yet thoughtful gift and break up with you the next day? Plus, looking at the big picture, if you start out with splurges, and then gradually offer smaller and cheaper ones, your partner could (with some justification) think that you're taking them for granted. Instead, start small and with a modest budget, and only invest big money in the relationship when it has stood the test of time and truly earned it.

Suitable, modest gifts for fledgling relationships are things like flowers, small pieces of costume jewelry, visits to restaurants and movies, and other items that are budget appropriate and meet your loved one's interests: a set of paints for a budding artist, the latest bestseller by their favorite author, or a new catcher's mitt for the avid baseball player.

Whatever gift you are given (and sadly, some people are just lousy at choosing gifts for others—it doesn't mean they're rude or thoughtless), you should always smile brightly and thank them graciously and sincerely (or as sincerely as you can) for the lovely item.

> PRO TIP: *If you genuinely don't know what an item is, the time to ask is shortly after opening it, not days later. It can feel embarrassing but it's by far the best policy to be honest. "Oh, thank you, how very thoughtful. Could I ask what it is? I've never seen anything so unusual like this before." This expresses your gratitude and allows them to explain to you exactly why it really is a thoughtful gift.*
>
> *If you're ever offered an impossibly expensive gift that you know you must refuse, the procedure is similar: "Thank you so much for this lovely pendant, but it's far too much. I can't possibly accept it, but I do thank you for the very kind thought."*

Chapter fourteen:
How to Be a Good Date

When you start dating your crush, you might feel giddy, excited, on top of the world, and overjoyed, longing to rush around and tell everyone about your amazing news! But hold off on announcing anything--just yet.

There is a lovely intimacy in being the only two who know you're dating during those precarious (and precious) first few days and dates, while you're still getting to know each other properly. Sometimes relationships don't survive these first few dates, and sometimes they're nipped in the bud by having too many interested parties intruding--making suggestions for gifts, date ideas, and more, or even just showing an interest.

Nurture your budding relationship by keeping it protected until you're both sure it can survive teasing, scrutiny, and the glare of publicity. During this time you will get to know each other and may uncover funny little quirks and foibles in your partner. These small, personal details are private and should never be shared with anyone outside the relationship, even if you're telling it as a positive (a cute thing they do). However, anything purely positive that they do, you absolutely can sing about to your friend group. Did they intervene to make a bully back off? They deserve hero status. Help a neighbor with a tricky repair job? Tell the world about their selflessness and special skills. But they have a fear of fruit rotting inside, and always slice it to make sure it's not? No, that's a private quirk and they will not thank you for sharing that.

If you are in a relationship and your partner begins to make demands on you that feel excessive or controlling, you should exercise a little caution around them. Many people, when hearing of abusive relationships—coercive control, bullying, even outright violence—can automatically assume a victim-blaming stance: "Why didn't they leave?" "No one will ever tell me what to do." "I wouldn't put up with that behavior."

Narcissists and bullies are well aware that people will not tolerate this behavior early in a relationship, and they'll play a game of being the perfect partner, thoughtful and kind, anticipating your every need and wish. But slowly, over time, once they think they have you in their pocket— "such a kind, sweet person, he/she would never hurt me!"—they begin to tighten their trap. It can start with "gaslighting" to make you doubt yourself.

"I asked you to meet me in town at two today. I'm really disappointed you weren't there."

"You didn't ask me to meet today, you said it would be next time!"

Smile, sigh forgivingly. "Did you get the date wrong again? You were a bit tired this morning, weren't you? Oh well, never mind. It's a good thing I love you, you know…"

Because this sort of thing is never allowed to be solved properly—the bully will always deflect any insistence that they're wrong, turning it into another fault on the other person's part— even the most strong-minded person will begin to have doubts about something that, deep down, they know for a fact. And slowly in this way, the bully takes control of the narrative and the other partner, constantly wrong-footed, becomes more and more certain they must have messed up and that they are in the wrong, that they are always in the wrong.

> FUN FACT: *Our brains are wired to constantly edit themselves. The idea that our brains work like a movie, perfectly creating a faultless record of events, is a very incorrect comparison. Instead, it's perfectly possible to persuade people that their memories are wrong, in favor of an edited story (we didn't go to Grandma's for lunch, it was Aunt Betty's for dinner), or even plant an entirely false memory of something that never happened ("Remember when we climbed to the top of the Statue of Liberty? You were wearing your blue shorts and got scared of the height"). Repeated often enough, eventually our brains will accept this as a truism and it will become your new memory despite not having been your actual experience. (This is why hypnotism and guided psychoanalysis are iffy fields, legally speaking. Are those "recovered" memories real, or have they been fabricated by our clever but very strange brains?) There is actually a word for these made-up but sincerely believed memories: confabulation.*

It's a scary thought, isn't it?

Recovering from such relationships can be tough, so learn to listen to and trust your instincts, and walk away as soon as you begin to feel that your loving partner is not so loving after all.

But hopefully your date will neither be a control freak nor a narcissist. And regular people are very easy to talk to and communicate with, as long as you learn how to do so in a mature manner.

Learn to express your thoughts and feelings in neutral ways that do not put blame on the other person or imply an expectation that they must change to suit your preferences. It might not feel like it, but this is a form of bullying. Every relationship has ups and downs: you might love the way they wrinkle their nose but dislike the sound of their chewing. You don't have the right to insist that they eat in seclusion to mitigate your dislike; it is your problem to deal with as best you can.

> FUN FACT: *A dislike of certain sounds—chewing, breathing, tapping, or clicking, and more— is called misophonia and is a recognized neurological condition. It is not a mere "dislike" of these sounds; it causes an extreme reaction, and the sufferer will become agitated and upset, perhaps even crying with frustration, or feeling the need to flee from the noise. Reaction to the triggering sound often presents as anger, and some misophonia sufferers insist that the fault doesn't lie with them but rather with the people making the noise. While good etiquette demands certain things that will naturally help a sufferer*

(eating with your mouth closed, for example, and not fidgeting about), it is, in fact, an extreme reaction to noises that are actually harmless and inoffensive, and really not an instance of rudeness or poor manners on the part of the "offending" party who is just living their life as best they can. The sufferer should be allowed to take steps to mitigate their upset (it is NOT temper or pettiness, they genuinely become distressed by these sounds) by playing music to cover the noise, using discreet earphones, or being allowed to move away from the incessantly ticking clock or tapping foot, rather than being called out for being intolerant or rude.

For example, if your partner always throws their coat over the couch instead of hanging it on a hook, this can be expressed neutrally: "Can I hang up your coat?" or "There's a free hook on the coatrack," rather than with blame: "Ugh! You always do that! Can't you hang up your coat?!" In any situation, put yourself in the other person's shoes, and think about how you'd like the situation handled.. What would make you amenable to changing the way you do things? And also consider if it—whatever "it" is—actually matters in the long run before you decide to mention it at all.

One thing that's important in a new relationship is to allow each other personal space. Make time for your friends, especially if you have a shared group of friends, but also if you have separate friends. Being apart from each other every now and then will make the time you spend together all the sweeter,("absence makes the heart grow fonder," right?), as well as giving you both something to talk about when you're together, and ensuring that any breakup will be more manageable because you'll have maintained interests and hobbies outside of the little world comprising just the two of you.

Chapter fifteen:
That First Date

Jumping back a little to that all-important first date: think about it carefully before committing to it. Choosing a venue that you love but that is otherwise a little niche—a monster truck show, or a designer shoe exhibition-—can be selfish. Instead, choose somewhere neutral, but still low-key fun for your first date or, better yet, let your date choose the agenda for the night so you can both express any strong dislikes before committing to it.

All first dates should take place in public places with an easy option for either of you to end the date early and head home if it's uncomfortable or doesn't seem to be working out. Plan the date in advance, and if your date wants to know the details, do tell them what you'll be doing even if you'd hoped for it to be a surprise. People—especially women or people with anxiety—do not like surprises in the early stages of relationships, preferring instead to know exactly what will be happening, from pickup or meeting point to final farewell at the end of the date. If your date expresses concern over any secrecy, indulge them by providing an agenda--where you'll be eating and which movie theater you'll be attending, even if you do want to keep the specific movie details a surprise to them.

> PRO TIP: *Some boys and men get offended when they realize that girls and women are taking steps to be safe while in their company. If you find yourself in this situation, do not take it personally. Instead, understand that females are subject to horrendous levels of abuse, which can range from the mild (unwanted whistles and catcalls) to much more serious problems. And at this stage, they still do not know you. You might be a decent person, but they don't know this yet, and until they've gotten better acquainted with you, they'll be cautious for their own sake.*

Once the venue and itinerary are planned, the next question to ask is how are you both getting there and back? Who'll be driving, and what time can you expect the date to finish? Whatever the plans are, always ensure there's a backup plan just in case something goes wrong or one of you wants to leave early for any reason.

The first date is an intimidating time to "meet the parents," but some will insist upon it. If you've managed to avoid meeting them so far, do try to meet them any time around the third month of the relationship. Leaving it any longer than this can make it seem as though you're dodging them, which will put most parents on their guard, making the first meeting a rather awkward and suspicious one.

When you do meet the parents, check with your partner beforehand as to their names— they might have different last names from your partner, for example—and use any titles they've earned, such as doctor, captain, and so on. Greet them politely and ask how their day or week has been, answering them politely and as fully as is appropriate when they ask about your family, your prospects and dreams, and any hobbies you might enjoy. You might feel as though you are being interrogated or interviewed—and you're completely right! That's exactly what they're doing. And they're perfectly within their rights. You are, after all, asking to be accepted as a near-family member and they want to know all about you before they let you into their home and their hearts.

On to the date itself. In general, the person who has issued the invite to the date is assumed to be paying for both, unless alternative arrangements have been made. If you do want to treat your date make this clear so there's no awkwardness, and definitely mention if you're expecting to "go Dutch," in which case each person pays for their own meal, movie ticket, etc.

> PRO TIP: *If you're going to suggest splitting the bill down the middle (which is never really a good idea) rather than each paying for what they've consumed, do not order the most expensive items on the menu while they are choosing the cheaper options. This is extremely tacky and unfair, and will almost certainly make your first date your last one.*

If you're invited to a very expensive restaurant that you know you would not be able to afford, be upfront about this. You don't have to go into detail about your anemic finances, just say something simple like, "Gosh, that's expensive, isn't it? I'm afraid I'll have to decline; my wallet won't allow that this month."

Similarly, even if you've been invited out on the date and your partner has every intention of paying for your meal, it is quite appropriate to insist on paying for your own meal, if you have legit reasons for doing so. Do not assume you're being rejected if your date insists on paying for their own meal; they can do so for any number of reasons from personal beliefs like not wanting to feel beholden to anyone. It does not mean they hate you and will block you as soon as they get home. If this happens, leave a large and generous tip, and offer to buy your date an ice cream or coffee as you stroll around after your meal. They are more likely to accept this small gesture, having seen your approval of their paying for their own meal.

Never have expectations about what should or should not happen on a first date. There is nothing more crushing to an early romance than feeling forced into something they're not comfortable with, whether this is a kiss or merely holding hands. The most you should hope for on your first date is for both of you to have a good time—*such* a good time that they're eager to repeat the experience by agreeing to a second date!

So far, this section has been a little dismaying, packed full of warnings, tips on how to behave that can seem impossible or contradictory, and more minefields than a war zone. But don't let all these cautions put you off because there's nothing more delightful than a first date that goes well.

Remember to treat your date with respect and kindness, and if they do the same for you it's all but guaranteed that you'll both have a great time. While having separate interests is great, finding someone who shares those interests with you is even better. Going on a date with someone with whom you have a lot in common will fly by as you chat and get to know one another better, setting your relationship off to a fine start.

SECTION SIX:
ONLINE ETIQUETTE

Chapter sixteen:
Written Manners

Emails, handwritten letters (which are still the "done thing" in certain circles, considered the peak of politeness, especially after someone has done something nice for you), and typed correspondence ("typed" here means something typed on a computer and printed to send), all still have their place in the world, even with the immediacy of messaging apps and social media.

Emails can be sent by almost anyone to anyone else: to confirm details of a meeting or holiday, catch-up with distant friends and family on your goings on, or simply touch base with people you haven't seen for a while and who live in a place where phone calls might be awkward, such as, on the other side of the world with large gaps in time zones. Emails will wait patiently to be read and answered without anyone needing to lose any sleep.

Handwritten letters or notes are the best way to thank people for hosting them, or for thoughtful gifts—even for awards given for whatever reason. Choose pretty or fine quality paper and use a lined page underneath to make sure your writing stays in even lines. Think about what you want to write and start again if you make a mistake that's ugly and obvious. It's a good idea to write your letter on a piece of scrap paper or on a device until you have a good first draft that reads well, and then carefully copy it out in your best handwriting.

Keep these letters short and sweet. Mention the event, say thank you for the gift (naming whatever the item is, such as "the lovely cardigan" or "delicious cookies"), and then close with a warm sign off.

Typed correspondence is usually used for business matters. This can include college applications, queries about loans and bursaries, as well as any other correspondence you need to compose.

Both emails and digital letters can be saved on the computer, so you have a record to refresh your memory, chase up the matter, or add extra details if you realize you've forgotten something.

With all of these forms of correspondence there are ways to acknowledge receipt. If you can't respond quickly, it's polite to send a response within a day or two, acknowledging receipt of their request or notice and letting them know when they can expect a full response. This is much easier to do by email as you can quickly hit "reply" and type a sentence or two. Once you've given yourself a little breathing room, make sure you respond as soon as you possibly can, preferably before the deadline in your acknowledgment.

In writing, if you know the person you can address them as you do on a daily basis: Auntie Jane, Grandma, Big Bro, etc. These letters and emails will almost always be informal, and you can adopt a folksy, friendly tone.

Semiformal, businesslike letters should be addressed to a specific person whenever possible, or to "Dear Sir or Madam" if you really have no idea who'll be opening your letter. You can also be more specific without knowing names: "Dear Admissions Officer," for example is acceptable if you have no other choice. But often, you'll be able to find the name of a college's admissions officer with a quick Internet search, so make sure you do your due diligence before reverting to anonymity.

Very formal letters should be addressed using the complete name of the person: "Mrs. Martha Jones," for example, and they should be as perfectly written and as grammatically correct as you can manage.

Thank-you notes should usually be handwritten, but a call or an email is acceptable too, and they should always be very brief. "Thank you so much for hosting me at your lovely holiday home in the Hamptons. I had a wonderful time and will always treasure my memories of this weekend"—literally two or three sentences, and they should be neatly penned if written by hand and use proper English without slang phrases or informal words. As well as thanking hosts for their hospitality, you should also write thank-you notes for gifts received, especially from people you don't know very well, or family members you don't see very often. Good etiquette demands that thank-you notes should be written as swiftly as possible—the night you received the gift, or the day you return from your visit—and sent quickly so your host receives them almost before they've had time to wonder if you had a good time or enjoyed the gift.

Chapter seventeen:
Netiquette

There is a very simple rule to remember regarding social media that will keep you out of trouble (almost) all the time: it is a public forum and people can see what you're saying and sharing. Assume that this is true, even if you're in a closed or private group chat. If you have more than one social media account on the same network, make sure you keep them separate. For example, you might have an account for your fan fiction or just for talking about your favorite television shows or book series, and another account so your family can share news and photos with each other. This way Grandma can comment on your family day at the beach, and your fellow fans can read your fan fiction without being able to see private information about you.

It can be tempting to screenshot (or otherwise save) embarrassing posts by others--but try to avoid this. No one likes being reminded of silly moments or accidental shares, and if they have deleted the original post it's almost certainly because they have realized that there's a problem with it and want to put it behind them. Allow people to move on from their mistakes, just as you would want to be allowed to move on from yours; there is not one person of the eight billion on the planet who has not or will not make some sort of mistake or *faux pas* at one point or another.

Screenshots should be used with care, usually only to preserve evidence of a crime or to capture a moment that really appeals to you, and that you'd like to treasure for your personal use, such as a motivational image or a heartwarming poem that speaks to you. And, strictly speaking, you really should ask the original poster for permission before saving their post.

Here are some more dos and don'ts of good social media netiquette:

- Don't share images of other people online, certainly not without their express permission. More and more people are controlling how much of their image is disseminated online, so avoid arguments and even legal disputes by not sharing any images without permission from identifiable people.

- Never share confidential information. Your friends and followers might be cool, but you only need one suspicious character to discover your address or what school you attend in order to find yourself in a world of fear and even the victim of stalking. Always be mindful that you're sharing a worldwide platform where any nefariously-minded person can disguise their identity to whatever and whomever they want to be.

- Try not to post random, meaningless quotes or images. Will you really want to see that burger and fries in your memories five, seven, or nine years from now? No? Then don't post it now.

- Do check facts. If your least favorite teacher or neighbor is suddenly shown in an image "proving" that they're as big an idiot as you've always thought, it's tempting to yell, "I knew it!" and reshare the image to all your followers. But even your worst enemy deserves the truth, not made-up, unpleasant lies, or falsified images. Unfortunately, the advent of AI (artificial intelligence) programs for both text and images have seen a huge spike in fake images or tweaks made to real images to make people look even worse or sillier than they actually are. As a result, real vigilance is needed to avoid propagating these falsehoods to your followers. To verify a public image or piece of information, always reverse image search, or look for that news on the mainstream media. Remember that individuals on social media posts and sites like Reddit and YouTube or TikTok are not held to any real degree of accountability and can easily "fake" stories and images to suit any narrative.

Just as you wouldn't go out into the street when you're feeling angry or emotional, nor should you enter social media platforms in that state. Remember that while it's good etiquette to allow people to erase their past mistakes and move on, there are also always those who screenshot posts that they think the poster might regret later. An ounce of prevention here is infinitely better than several pounds of cure because things on the Internet can be forever, and you don't want your puerile posts from your teen years coming back to haunt you in your twenties, thirties, and forties just as you stand on the brink of success.

Good social media visibility, however, can help "future you" with your dreams and plans. Colleges and workplaces often trawl through social media looking for more information and details about prospective hires or students, and having a well-curated, sensible feed can tip the balance in your favor should you be in a tie with another candidate whose social media platform is not as well maintained.

Online, a whole alphabet of symbols and indications have sprung up.

> FUN FACT: *Linguists are studying the evolution of "textspeak" as people all over the world seem to intuitively understand nuances and messages that are implicit and never explained. An example would be the difference between a reply of "Okay" versus "Okay." with a period after the word. The second version is instinctively understood to be passive-aggressive and slightly negative, as though the responder is not in agreement with the sender but doesn't want to make a big deal about it, while still expressing that subtle doubt. That's quite a hefty message to be contained in a single dot!*

In general, depending on your recipient, you should use plain text with easily understood emojis if strangers will be reading your messages. Despite the nuances mentioned above, it can be hard to get context from bald text even if it's accompanied by emojis, and an expression of ironic sympathy can come across as mocking to someone who is not familiar with your way of texting or messaging (or sense of humor). It is, of course, a different story with your friend group where you are firstly, sure to understand each other's shorthand and emoji intentions, and secondly, have more leeway as friends will ask you if you meant to sound mean or cold about something, giving you the chance to clarify your intentions.

WRITING IN ALL CAPS IS SHOUTING! Usually, anyway. Avoid shouting at people on social media unless you're telling a joke or doing it for easily discernible, ironic reasons. But try to keep it to a minimum to avoid people becoming upset with you for yelling at them all the time. People have adapted so well to text communications that their brains actually register the same discomfort on seeing all-caps messages as they do when actively being yelled at.

If you do share someone's work on social media, whether from their own post or from somewhere else—even if you commissioned them to create the piece for you—give them credit as the creator. It's a small gesture of thanks from you, but it can boost their profile and help them to succeed, and besides, it's always nice to be nice.

Chapter eighteen:
Texting

Texting is a relatively new method of communication and, as mentioned in the previous chapter, it seems to be largely instinctive with emojis, slang, and shorthand expressions all springing up, and things like the receipt of one-letter answers ("k") seen as passive-aggressive or rude. There is also the above-mentioned use of periods to convey sarcasm or annoyance (introducing passive-aggressive punctuation). Despite this thriving informal "language" growing up around texting, there are also rules of etiquette governing texting just as in other areas of life.

In groups on social media, care should be taken to only use the group to talk about group activities: if two or three members have their own event going on, they should set up a separate group chat just for themselves. Most messaging apps such as Snapchat, Instagram, TikTok, and others allow for group messages, so most people will be able to make use of group chats to arrange events, share homework information, or simply keep up-to-date with each other.

One thing group chats should not be used for is asking for money toward things like arranging a birthday gift for a mutual friend. It's better, by far, to individually message each friend in the group, asking if they want to contribute and how much they can put into the kitty rather than assume that everyone can afford a large sum. Financial embarrassment can be mortifying to young people (and even to some older people too) who struggle to express the fact that their income is perhaps not as large as others.

Despite messenger apps being the epitome of instant gratification, we send and receive so many of them each day that it can become overwhelming, especially if we mute our phone for a couple of hours and come back to find hundreds of messages on a group thread. Do try to respond to messages within twenty-four hours, and if you're unable to do this let them know when you will offer a "proper" response. You can also "like" a message to show that you've read it. You don't have to respond with words if it doesn't seem necessary. But texts are designed for your convenience, more so than phone calls which demand instant responses, so you can finish what you're doing, think of an appropriate response, and then reply when you're ready.

Even though texts are extremely convenient, there are some occasions that warrant a phone call or even an in-person visit. Breakups, news of a bereavement (any bad news, in fact, as well as good news—promotions, the birth of a baby, or a successful house move) should all be done by a phone call or in-person so that the person receiving the news can react to it in real time, and if necessary, the person breaking the bad news can dole out some comfort and solace to them.

Phone calls are somewhat repugnant to the generation that has been raised with text messaging available from birth. Phone calls are rude, intrusive, and insistent on an immediate answer, whereas texts can be read and absorbed at your own pace and replied to once you have time to word it correctly and respond appropriately. However, even with this modern sensibility, sometimes phone calls—or even video calls—are a necessity.

The best way to ensure your phone call is answered is to send a text before the call saying that you'll be calling and when, giving the recipient time to read the message and (hopefully) acknowledge it. Do let them know what the call will be about so they know not to worry: "Calling you about my job, will phone in about twenty minutes," for example, lets them know that their family members are all safe, and they might even be able to surmise that you got the job or the promotion you were hoping for!

FUN FACTS: *What do these acronyms mean: idk, idc, iirc, afaik?* And did you know your great-grandparents had similar notations: SWALK written across a sealed letter meant "sealed with a loving kiss." Flowers, too, had a range of meanings: red roses for love, yellow for remembrance, and so on. (*Answers: I don't know; I don't care; if I recall correctly; as far as I know.)*

With any kind of technology, especially if it sends and receives notifications, try to turn it off during special occasions and important events. Being mindfully present and paying attention to the people around you are very simple ways to demonstrate your grasp of good etiquette.

When sending messages and memes, bear in mind your recipient's frame of reference and temperament. Don't send inappropriate content to adults such as your friends' parents, make sure your grandparents will understand any "edgy" references, and—as always—if you're in any doubt, don't send it at all!

Finally, remember to check the time before hitting "send" on that green phone or message. As a rule of thumb, avoid contacting others between 9 p.m. and 9 a.m. as this is when many people are getting ready for bed, sleeping, or going through their morning routine—none of which are good times to be disturbed.

SECTION SEVEN:
BUILD A "FUTURE YOU" TO BE PROUD OF

Chapter nineteen:
Mindful You

Your teenage years are a time of tremendous upheaval. Your body, temperament, tastes, and more are all changing almost constantly during this time, and even comparisons with friends can leave you confused and worried. For example, when the person who has always been shorter than you suddenly shoots up, while you remain stubbornly at your current height these things can be very worrying. Remember, the teenage brain is wired to experience everything at extremes of emotion, making your joys sweeter and your sadness even more sorrowful.

Learning some coping mechanisms will be your friend during your turbulent teens, and these skills can be carried over into your adult life too. Hitting your twenties with a conscious mindfulness and the ability to control and direct your emotions can be an enormous plus! But, in the here and now, what is mindfulness and how can you achieve it?

Mindfulness is simply being conscious of the here and now. How are you feeling? What is your breathing like? Are you tense or relaxed? Be aware of what's going on around you instead of worrying about the test you had earlier, or the exam results you'll be getting tomorrow—exist in the present. Meditation is a great way to achieve mindfulness, and it can be as simple as sitting comfortably with your eyes closed if you prefer, and focusing on yourself. Breathe in and out deliberately and slowly, and with each exhale empty your mind a little more. Get rid of those school issues, concerns about your looks, worries about getting into a good college—throw them all out on a breath. Do this for a few minutes, then when you've cleared your mind of all the "clutter," simply continue sitting for five or ten minutes, thinking about nothing but your breathing, the feel of the air against your body, muscles, and bones—all of which should be nicely relaxed.

If this doesn't work for you, you can sign up for more formal and physical types of meditation, such as, yoga or tai chi in which you'll be guided through mental exercises even as your body is stretched and contorted.

Journaling is another great way to achieve mindfulness. The act of writing is also an act of thinking, and sometimes merely writing down your dreams and aspirations can help to firm and center them in your psyche. This means that if you write down aspirational thoughts like, "I am a great actor at the peak of my powers" or "I am strong and fit and can run five miles in fifteen minutes," they can not only help you to understand your goals and begin to work for them, but you can also persuade your subconscious that you have, in fact, already achieved them! And having "achieved" your goals mentally by manifesting them then genuine success will not be too far behind. This is a very powerful technique that will help you form a growth mindset that'll carry throughout your life.

Journaling is similar to keeping a diary, but it's more targeted and businesslike, which tends to be a retelling of what happened during the day. Journaling can be done in just a few minutes at the beginning or end of the day (or perhaps both, setting up targets for the day and then reporting on them later). There are hundreds of different layouts to choose from, but you can always get a blank journal and organize it the way that works best for you. Most will have areas for making to-do lists, spaces for organizing your day, and sections where you can reaffirm your goals and notate progress toward them. Include mantras that you want to remember: "I can achieve my goals if I work diligently towards them," "Slow progress is still progress, I will get there!", and so on.

If you are one of those people whose anxieties and worries seem to swell and infect everything else, you're not alone, and these worries can be managed! Write down your concerns. Often this is enough to make them seem more distant, smaller than they'd seemed in your head, and much more manageable.

> **PRO TIP:** *Share genuine worries by saying them aloud to someone you trust. Not only might they be able to help you find a solution because they have a different viewpoint on the matter, but the simple act of expressing a worry out loud works to temper even the most serious problem. Not for nothing is there a saying that, "A trouble shared is a trouble halved." This works, even if the person you tell doesn't have any ideas to help you. The mere act of expressing your worry works to reduce it.*

Daily Intentions & Reflections

Morning

Word of the Day: Start your day by choosing one word to set the tone.

To-Do List: Note down three primary tasks you intend to complete today.

Daily Mantra: Choose or write a mantra to inspire and guide you today.

Evening

Achievements: Reflect on what you accomplished today.

Progress Towards Goals: Note any small or large progress made toward your long-term objectives.

Gratitude: Write down one thing you're thankful for from the day.

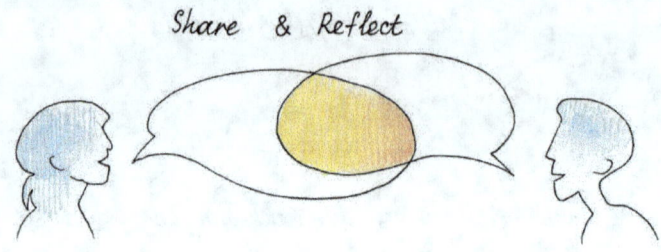

Shared Concerns

Document any worries or issues you shared with someone today.

Received Feedback

Note down any insights, feedback, or alternate perspectives given by the person you confided in. Even if they didn't have solutions, remember, sharing itself is therapeutic.

Reflection

Reflect on how sharing these concerns made you feel. Did expressing them out loud make the worries feel smaller? Was there relief in sharing?

Worries & Solutions

My Worries Today

List down concerns or anxieties you have today. Sometimes just writing them makes them feel less overwhelming.

Possible Solutions or Actions

For each worry you've listed, try to think of one possible solution or a step you can take to address or reduce that concern.

We live ridiculously busy lives these days, and it can be all too hard to find a spare moment. Think about your day in a new way, looking not for hours, but for minutes. Five minutes while you wait for class to start; fifteen minutes on the bus; think through homework problems while you do sports or walk home (thinking about the ways to solve homework questions gives you a head start when you finally sit down to tackle the problem with pen and paper); make your lunch sandwiches two- and three-days' worth at a time, and learn the art of "good laziness." Good laziness is not about doing things badly or haphazardly and having to redo them. Good laziness is all about finding the quickest, most effective way of completing a task without the need for repeating it —a most efficient use of your time!

When you're first trying to live mindfully, and perhaps adding journaling or meditation into an already packed schedule, monitor your time usage for a day or two. Do you snooze your alarm three times in the morning, so you actually get up half an hour after you're meant to? Does "just one episode" of your favorite show turn into an all-afternoon binge? How much time exactly does it take to read all those fascinating listicles and scroll through social media posts?

Once you've seen how much time you're wasting, you can maybe claw some of it back and put it to good use by doing homework, learning a language, playing a sport, joining an after school club, or even just spending it with family and friends.

We all have the same hours in a day—make the best possible use of yours!

Chapter twenty:
Planning for Future Work

Schoolchildren today—you, in other words—will almost certainly grow up to work in jobs that do not yet exist. This means that your future is uncertain as highly in-demand positions *now* are sure to become obsolete in as few as five years, and new, equally in-demand positions will be opening up—or being opened up by enterprising youth.

So, it's hard to understand what you should study to give yourself the best chance for success and satisfaction. If you don't know what the future holds, how can you possibly prepare for it?

However, there are some things you can work on developing. These will come in handy in any future:
- Creativity: the ability to think "outside the box" is what keeps new products and services flowing into the market, and creativity is something uniquely human. While AI programs seem to show signs of creativity, most of the "art" they produce is derivative, formed by

examining hundreds and thousands of existing pieces of art and copying traits and features to produce something "unique".

- Emotional Intelligence or EQ: the ability to understand the other point of view or perspective, or to feel and show empathy towards others. Not only is this a great management tool found in all good leaders, but it will give you self-confidence, which will also help you in your future career endeavors.

- Critical thinking: a sorely lacking commodity in a world in which common sense is no longer very common. Critical thinking is the ability to assess given information and deduce whether it's credible or not, important or not, or even to realize that it is carefully crafted misinformation designed to make trouble. Work on your critical thinking skills and they will stand you in very good stead your whole life. Having good critical thinking skills will impart to you good judgment, so you'll easily be able to spot scams or deceptions.

It's a scientific fact that teenage brains are complex, transforming dramatically from a child's brain into an adult's brain—a process that takes until about the age of twenty-five to complete when the frontal cortex (the seat of reason and good judgment) is finally fully developed. But this also means that teens are uniquely able to learn fast and well, so you should make the most of any learning opportunities that come your way. Expanding your comfort zone and adopting a growth mindset can prepare you for an anxiety-free and safely adventurous adulthood.

A growth mindset is what people in the sixties would have called a "can-do attitude." Trying new things, being willing to make mistakes and look a bit foolish before trying again and finally getting it right, and telling oneself that, "I can do this!" are all evidence of a growth mindset. The opposite involves giving into anxieties, refusing to try, or folding at the first difficulty. It's easy to see that such teens will be fearful and anxious with a shrunken comfort zone most likely comprising their homes and schools and not much else.

The love of learning—and ensuring you keep learning throughout your whole life—is the best way to foster a growth mindset. Don't worry if you struggle to learn from a teacher reading notes to you. This may simply mean that you learn a different way. There are three or four ways of learning: some learn best by reading information, others by hearing it read and explained to them, yet others learn by doing the things explained. Most of us combine two or more of these ways of learning. For example, hearing it and writing it down is effective for those who learn best by "reading"—they "read" what they're writing, which reinforces the "weak" learning spot by solely the spoken words. Others might like to be talked through an experiment; hearing the instructions as they complete each step helps them learn the topic. Find your best way of learning and embrace it, indulging your interests and passions. Who knows, in the fast-changing world of work, one of your interests might turn out to kick-start a long and successful career!

Other things you should try to learn while you're still young are:

- Good communication skills (being a good and mindful listener who can also be a persuasive speaker when necessary).

- How to manage projects and people.

- How to implement management practices.

- Gaining knowledge and understanding of diversity and inclusivity practices.

- Embracing new technologies.

- Developing cultural intelligence (embracing and understanding the differences of other people without making them feel like outsiders).

- Being ready, at all times, to adapt and change along with advances and improvements in practices and habits!

> FUN FACT: *The world has "revolutions" from time to time that you might have learned about in class, such as, the Industrial Revolution and the Agricultural Revolution. However, we're currently in the middle of another revolution: the "Technological" Revolution, which has completely changed the way we live, work, and play (and learn), with immense changes over the last hundred years, and in particular during the last ten years or so. Who knows what revolutions you will experience during your lifetime.*

And that brings us to the end of this little book on etiquette and how to be the very best that you can be. Good luck for your future and remember at all times that with your newfound understanding of etiquette the world is your oyster—just make sure that you use the appropriate fork when indulging in this delicacy!

THE AUTHOR

At the tender age of three, Alla had already begun a tutelage in social mores and manners at an educational daycare in the Ukraine run by etiquette professionals where she learned the importance of making eye contact, polite greetings, and the basics of dining and table manners. She continued formal etiquette training throughout her childhood and teen years, making several pit stops at esteemed manners and boarding schools throughout Europe, receiving a merit/honors diploma as an etiquette teacher at a prestigious British school where she graduated as an etiquette coach, then mastered the skills of flag etiquette, international relations, high-level delegation visits and conferences in Haag. Alla completed her formal global training on the finer points of American decorum and the cultural differences from continental protocols in New York City. To Alla, founder of the Lluxxall School of Etiquette and Manners in San Diego, geared for children and teens, enriching students on the basics of decorum from the dining room, classroom, and dorm room to the computer room and eventually boardroom is a natural and organic passion and her life's mission. Coupled with an online advice column for teens, numerous magazine articles, live talks, podcasts, and now this compelling and comprehensive handbook, Alla will be repairing the world by molding a future generation of refined, self-confident, and well-mannered students well-equipped to achieve happiness and success both personally and professionally.

www.ingramcontent.com/pod-product-compliance
Lightning Source LLC
Chambersburg PA
CBHW052142070526
44585CB00017B/1937